teach®
yourself

how to write a
blockbuster
lee weatherly and
helen corner

For over 60 years, more than
50 million people have learnt over
750 subjects the **teach yourself**
way, with impressive results.

be where you want to be
with **teach yourself**

For UK order enquiries: please contact Bookpoint Ltd, 130 Milton Park, Abingdon, Oxon, OX14 4SB. Telephone: +44 (0) 1235 827720. Fax: +44 (0) 1235 400454. Lines are open 09.00–17.00, Monday to Saturday, with a 24-hour message answering service. Details about our titles and how to order are available at www.teachyourself.co.uk

For USA order enquiries: please contact McGraw-Hill Customer Services, PO Box 545, Blacklick, OH 43004-0545, USA. Telephone: 1-800-722-4726. Fax: 1-614-755-5645.

For Canada order enquiries: please contact McGraw-Hill Ryerson Ltd, 300 Water St, Whitby, Ontario, L1N 9B6, Canada. Telephone: 905 430 5000. Fax: 905 430 5020.

Long renowned as the authoritative source for self-guided learning – with more than 50 million copies sold worldwide – the **teach yourself** series includes over 500 titles in the fields of languages, crafts, hobbies, business, computing and education.

British Library Cataloguing in Publication Data: a catalogue record for this title is available from the British Library.

Library of Congress Catalog Card Number: on file.

First published in UK 2006 by Hodder Education, 338 Euston Road, London NW1 3BH.

First published in US 2006 by The McGraw-Hill Companies, Inc.

This edition published 2006.

The **teach yourself** name is a registered trade mark of Hodder Headline.

Typeset by Transet Limited, Coventry, England.
Printed in Great Britain for Hodder Education, a division of Hodder Headline, 338 Euston Road, London, NW1 3BH, by Cox & Wyman Ltd, Reading, Berkshire.

The publisher has used its best endeavours to ensure that the URLs for external websites referred to in this book are correct and active at the time of going to press. However, the publisher and the author have no responsibility for the websites and can make no guarantee that a site will remain live or that the content will remain relevant, decent or appropriate.

Hodder Headline's policy is to use papers that are natural, renewable and recyclable products and made from wood grown in sustainable forests. The logging and manufacturing processes are expected to conform to the environmental regulations of the country of origin.

Impression number   10 9 8 7 6 5 4 3
Year   2010 2009 2008 2007

the authors

Part one written by Lee Weatherly
Part two (and foreword) written by Helen Corner

Helen Corner

With a background in publishing, Helen is the founder of Cornerstones and Kids' Corner, a leading UK literary consultancy. Essentially an editing house that works on shaping manuscripts with authors, agents and publishers, it is also known for launching over 40 new writers. With Lee Weatherly as the primary consultant, Helen runs a popular series of writing and self-editing workshops, and online tutorials.

www.cornerstones.co.uk

Lee Weatherly

With a background in agenting, Lee has written award-winning fiction for teenagers. Her first novel, *Child X*, was a category winner of the 2003 Sheffield Children's Book Award, and her novel *Missing Abby* was shortlisted for the 2005 Edgar Allan Poe Award in the US. Now a full-time writer, she works within a range of commercial genres as a freelance editor and consultant for Cornerstones. She is currently writing a novel for adults.

www.leeweatherly.com

iv

contents

acknowledgements

Many thanks are due to the authors, agents, editors and publishers who very generously gave of their time to answer our questionnaires. Their answers were illuminating and candid, and we only wish we had the space to use all of them.

Veronique Baxter, David Higham Associates
Jane Bidder
Malorie Blackman
Linda Chapman
Catherine Clarke, Felicity Bryan Literary Agency
Stephen Clarke
David Fickling, David Fickling Books
Richard Fitt, Authors Online
Katie Flynn
Clare Foss, Hodder
Adele Geras
Annette Green, Annette Green Authors' Agency
Kate Harrison
Maxine Hitchcock, HarperCollins
Mary Hoffman
Tanja Howarth, Tanja Howarth Literary Agency
Liz Kessler
Katherine Langrish
Kate Long
Carole Matthews
Barbara Nadel
Linda Newbery
Meg Rosoff
Nick Sayers, Hodder

Caroline Sheldon, Caroline Sheldon Literary Agency
Michael Marshall Smith
Philippa Milnes-Smith, LAW Ltd
G. P. Taylor

Philip Pullman's website quotes used courtesy of AP Watt Ltd.

Quote from David Gemmell's novel *Waylander* used courtesy of
the Howard Morhaim Literary Agency.

dedication

For every writer who aspires to be published

foreword

There's something incredibly exciting about picking up a manuscript and realizing that the author has natural talent. Shaping that talent and helping the author to the next stage is the foundation of what I do.

This excitement was sparked from my time as an assistant at Penguin ten years ago, where part of my job was to process unsolicited manuscripts. There was an automatic rejection policy in place, so most manuscripts were sent back with a standard note to the author. However, on occasion, there would be the odd manuscript that glinted with promise. One was *Past Imperfect* by John Matthews, a pacy psychological thriller, and a shiver of excitement snaked through me as I realized I was reading something special. It didn't fit the lists I worked for – Viking and Hamish Hamilton – so I passed it through to Michael Joseph, the commercial imprint of Penguin. John had been published before, but had been out of the loop for ten years, and so was feeling less than confident. He knew he had a great story, but despite all his efforts he was finding it hard to get noticed. When Michael Joseph offered him a two-book deal it was just desserts; better still, when it was published a year later and hit the best-seller list he was truly back on track.

John's manuscript needed little attention, and I'm sure it would have been picked up eventually. But this made me wonder about those manuscripts that were a little less polished and perhaps not so obvious. I would sometimes come across a gem in the pile that wouldn't be right for the imprints I worked for, but with a tweak here and there could perhaps be right for another list or publisher. Perhaps the opening pages were too slow, or chapter two should be in place of chapter one, the character or setting might not be established quickly or well enough, or the style might be mainly 'tell not show'. Usually, other than a quick scribble of encouragement, I wouldn't have time to tell the author any of this as I sent back the sample material with the standard rejection card.

Discovering John's manuscript and other 'nearly there' works in the slush pile inspired me to set up Cornerstones, and then later on Kids' Corner, as a way to give authors this essential feedback. Years on, with a 60-plus team of readers who are all professional authors or editors, we provide editorial feedback in the form of editorial reports and run workshops and tutorials on writing and self-editing. As a secondary part of our service, I also scout for agents, and pass on any of our authors who have real promise. I have been lucky enough to see a significant number of our authors go on to acquire an agent or publisher, and these are just the ones I know about – sometimes authors contact me years later telling me they got published!

When authors first begin to write it is often likened to falling in love. It is this creative energy that is perhaps the lifeblood to sparkling writing. However, they then have to get savvy and perfect what they have. One author, Jane Yardley, always comes to mind, as I think her hard-graft (and yet ultimately rewarding) writing experience epitomizes what many new writers must go through.

Jane travelled all over the world as a managing director to a pharmaceutical company, and in the empty hours of waiting in hotel rooms and airports, she wrote her first novel, *Painting Ruby Tuesday*. She wasn't sure what to do with it next, so before approaching agents or publishers she came to Cornerstones for some editorial feedback. It was a novel that flashed with brilliance, yet dulled in other places.

From the first editorial report I knew that I might want to submit this, but Jane first had to learn and apply the process of self-editing. She needed to look at her story objectively – using our report as a brainstorming tool – and then revise it to a submittable first draft. Two years on and many redrafts later I passed her through to the literary agency David Higham Associates, and she went on to get a healthy publishing deal.

Jane is a talented writer, but she needed to learn how to craft her writing skills. She told me that this learning process was often utterly frustrating and at times she thought she would never make it. She sheepishly confessed to me once that she was so upset her manuscript wasn't ready to submit that she chucked our first editorial report in the bin. She then fished it out 24 hours later and started redrafting. Over time, the self-editing process began to make sense. She is now on her third book and her skills are polished enough to no longer need us. She believes that if she'd submitted her novel in the state it was in when it originally came to us it would not have been taken on. I happen to believe that great writing will eventually make it, but I also know that the author has to work hard at perfecting it.

When Lee Weatherly first came to me as a reader, I knew that not only was she a talented writer but she was also one of the best editors and teachers I'd come across: thorough, clear and creative. Alongside her now award-winning writing career, Lee set up Kids' Corner for me and then went on to run our self-editing workshops for children's and adult writers. We both believe that the combined process of writing and self-editing is the key to creating excellent fiction, and this is what we aim to impart in our editorial feedback and in the workshops. In fact, it was our experience after one of these workshops – hearing the buzz and hum of writers swapping newly learned techniques – that led to us to write this book. If our workshop authors were continually telling us that what they had learned was like a light-bulb going on, then perhaps other writers would find these same techniques useful, too.

While this book isn't prescriptive to producing a blockbuster – after all, a book only becomes one once it begins to sell successfully – it does aim to explore how to write sparkling commercial fiction, and then how to submit it to agents and publishers in a professional way. You should always aim high and strive to perfect what you have, for although talent can't be taught, it can be honed and shaped. The good news is that these vital writing, self-editing and submission skills *can* be taught … and produce results.

I do hope that by reading this book it goes some way to demystifying the writing and publishing processes and that, most importantly, you find this a fun and positive journey and that I see your books on the shelves one day.

Helen Corner

part one

writing a blockbuster

01

getting started

In this chapter you will learn:
- how to choose a genre for your work
- how to establish the best physical environment, mental state and support network for your writing
- how to set yourself goals.

There are many reasons why you might want to be published. Making a living at something you love is probably high on your list, along with wanting your stories to reach readers. You might also want to feel validated as a writer, or simply to see your name in print alongside authors whose books you admire.

These are all good reasons for wanting to be published, but what should you write?

Perhaps you know the answer instantly. Or you may be wavering between several genres, unsure what direction you should go in. There are so many different types of fiction out there, each representing a different possible route for your career. Which one should you choose?

Let's start with what you shouldn't write:

- a book that you know is going to be a massive hit, because it's so much like another massive hit that's already been published
- a book that you think will be easy to write, such as a romance novel or children's fiction (think again)
- a book that you know will be huge, because you've already worked out the marketing presentation and cuddly toy buy-ins for it.

The problem with the above books – and agents turn down dozens of these every day – is that the only reason they're written is because the authors want to get published. Yes, I know that all writers want to get published (including you); that's a given. But you should never try to craft a story based solely on what you think is marketable; it's almost certain to be a dull, lifeless read. For any work of fiction to succeed, the author has to be its biggest fan.

New writers are often told to 'write what you know', but part of the fun of writing is to get away from our usual lives. If nobody did this, we wouldn't have any fantasy or science fiction. 'Write what you love' is much more pertinent. If you're fascinated by the Scott expedition to the South Pole, for example, don't feel that you shouldn't write about it because you weren't actually there or can't afford to travel. Research can make up for a lot (the Internet is a brilliant resource for writers), and nothing can replace an author's genuine excitement in a subject.

I never set out to write a best-seller. I wrote a novel I wanted to read, one that it seemed to me was missing from the market.

Kate Long

Michele Paver, whose teenage novel *Wolf Brother* sold for an unprecedented million pounds (the highest ever for a children's novel at time of print), has been enamoured with the distant past for most of her life. She did years of research on the subject before she even thought of writing a book, simply because she found it fascinating – and so when she did write *Wolf Brother*, the story had a spark of realism and enthusiasm that couldn't be faked. Perhaps there isn't a subject that you've spent years researching, but we all have themes or situations that interest us keenly. These are your raw materials; don't discount them. A good idea, executed with passion, counts for far more than something that's technically marketable but flat and lifeless.

Choosing a genre

What genre is right for you? The answer will almost always lie in the genre or genres that you most love to read. Do you read historical fiction voraciously? Are you an avid fantasy fan? These are the genres you should think seriously about writing in. You're already excited by the ideas of this particular genre, you're familiar with its conventions and, in terms of marketing research, you already have a good idea of what's being published – which story ideas have been done to death, common themes, and so on.

If your heart is set on writing a type of fiction that you're not familiar with, then the best advice I can give you is not to start writing for at least six months. Use that time to read everything in that genre you can get your hands on, so that when you do start to write, you're approaching your work with a solid knowledge of such genre standards as word count and overdone subject matter. While books such as this one can give you a brief overview of the different types of fiction, absolutely nothing can replace becoming familiar with your chosen genre yourself.

Sometimes new writers are reluctant to read what's currently being published in their area of fiction, as they're afraid of 'tainting' their own work, and want their ideas to be 'totally original'. It's fair enough to avoid a particular type of story while you're writing a first draft (I personally stay away from fiction similar to my own while writing), but to avoid familiarizing yourself with your genre beforehand is folly. Far from ensuring that your story is original, it's likely to result in one that's woefully out of style or has already been seen a hundred times. Do your research, and know your genre.

Read the works of other authors in your field. The great masters didn't get there overnight – they spent years in apprenticeships, learning from their masters before painting their own original masterpieces.

Clare Foss, Hodder Headline

It's worth being aware of the fact that publishers often expect authors to continue writing in the same genre once they're published, as it's much easier to market an author who keeps to a particular type of story. (An understandable point of view on their part: we all know the disappointment of reading a new book by a favourite author, only to find that she's gone off in a completely different direction.) Successful writers do write in different genres at times – Iain Banks comes to mind – but it's the exception rather than the rule, as it takes time and energy to build a following in more than one genre.

This isn't to say that you must be wedded to your chosen genre for life, but it's something to consider if you're currently the sort of author who dabbles in all sorts of stories, as a sort of 'playing the odds' way of trying to get published. ('I'll send my sci-fi novel out this week, and if they don't like that I'll try my children's novel, and if they don't like *that*, I'll send my thriller.') Try to think beyond the initial thrill of getting a contract. If you're published in one of these genres, you may find yourself writing that type of story for the next few years – so be careful to only submit work in areas of fiction where you'd be happy to do this. (See 'How you can build on your writing career' in Chapter 12 for further information on this.)

Finding time

New writers are sometimes under the misconception that they must take a sabbatical from work or even quit their jobs in order to find the time to write their novel, but this doesn't have to be the case. However, writing does take time, and this can be tricky to deal with when you're first starting out – most new writers must, by necessity, have full-time jobs outside of writing in order to deal with such pesky things as buying groceries and paying the mortgage. In addition, most of us have busy lives. It's not always easy to find quiet time to yourself, especially if you have children. But if you're serious about writing as a career, then there are no two ways around it: you must be disciplined about your writing time.

Make the promise to yourself that you'll write for at least half an hour every day. An hour is better if you can manage it, but half an hour is much better than nothing. Choose the time that's best for you, and then put that time in your diary as an appointment with yourself and keep it, no matter what. Close out all external distractions during this time: turn off the phone and ignore your email. It may feel strange at first, but once you've done it a few times, your writing time will become an ingrained habit (not to mention an addictive pleasure!) and you'll move mountains to make sure you've got your writing time every day.

However, don't make the mistake of waiting for inspiration to strike before you sit down to write. Sometimes (maybe even often) you won't feel like writing until you actually sit down and start to do it, and then suddenly you'll realize that you're totally involved and the time has flown past. But this magic won't happen if you don't give it the chance. Show up for your writing every day without any distractions, whether you think you're in the mood for it or not.

> All writing is difficult. The most you can hope for is a day when it goes reasonably easily. Plumbers don't get plumber's block, and doctors don't get doctor's block; why should writers be the only profession that gives a special name to the difficulty of working, and then expects sympathy for it?
>
> Philip Pullman

What about your family and friends, though? Just as you need to make writing your daily habit, you need to make it their habit to leave you in peace during that time. Consistent reactions from you will speak volumes: except in cases of real emergency, your writing time must be sacred.

Finding a space

The great thing about writing is that you can do it anywhere, especially if you have a laptop or write by hand. However, it's also good to have a particular spot in your home that's dedicated to writing. Having a special place to write in will help you take your writing seriously, and when you enter this space it will also act as a signal to your unconscious that now is the time to write.

A room with a door that can shut out the rest of the world is the best choice if you have the space, but it's not vital – any quiet place where you can be alone with your thoughts will do. The important thing is to find a spot that works for you and to be consistent about using it, be it a corner in your lounge or a desk in the spare bedroom.

You'll be spending a lot of time in this space, so make sure it's one that you feel comfortable in. If you're using a computer, make sure the screen is at eye level (you shouldn't have to tilt your head down at all to see the screen). Gel pads to rest your wrists on as you type are also a good idea. And, if you can afford it, it's worth investing in a good chair – and by that I mean a chair with proper isotonic support, rather than one of those big leather captain's chairs! Writers are very prone to back aches and repetitive strain injuries, so take what steps you can to avoid these.

You might also want to have a few objects around you that you find soothing or inspirational – for instance, on my desk there are several attractive stones that I found on the beach, along with some favourite photos – but don't get so carried away by decorating your writing space that you forget the most important thing: writing in it. A plain desk in a bare room would do the job just fine, if not better than a space so filled with decorative clutter that you can't think.

Although your writing space is probably where you'll do most of your work, writing in different places occasionally can give you fresh ideas and inspirations. If you feel things going a bit stale, try taking a notebook to the local coffee shop or pub, or writing under a tree in the park, or just sitting at the kitchen table for a change.

Writing goals

Should you set yourself writing goals, such as writing a certain number of pages per day? This can be a good idea for several reasons. A writing goal can help you to:

- signal to yourself that you're taking your writing seriously
- establish a regular writing routine
- move forward with a project rather than fiddling endlessly with the same few chapters.

Different writers set themselves different types of goals. I know a writer who draws up elaborate charts showing her weekly word count targets, and another who simply writes ten pages a day, regardless of how many words are on the pages (she admits that she cheats somewhat by using lots of snappy dialogue). Personally, I go by word count on a daily basis. There's no right or wrong way; it comes down to your own preference and what works best for you.

However, make sure you don't set yourself a target that's so high it's impossible for you; you'll only become discouraged. Check your word or page count over several days' writing to get an idea of your average output, and then make your goal just a little bit higher than that to stretch yourself. If you find yourself meeting this target effortlessly, increase it again. My daily word count has become steadily greater over the years as I've become a more practised writer.

Don't become obsessed by this, though. There are some days when, for whatever reason, you are simply not going to meet your goal. Sometimes real life intrudes; sometimes the muse is just being stubborn and refuses to be coaxed. If this happens, stop writing and do something else. You'll be amazed at how often a story problem will solve itself if you put your mind onto other things.

> You have to learn when (and how) to push yourself, and when to just walk away. Some days it's good to keep at it, but on others you'll just be making things worse and making yourself bored with what you've already got. It's all very well being a genius, but if you can't actually get the words down on paper reliably, no one's ever going to know.
>
> Michael Marshall Smith

To keep your writing momentum going from day to day, try stopping your day's writing mid-flow, right in the middle of that exciting scene you're having so much fun with. You'll be eager to return to it the next day, and when you begin to write you'll plunge easily back into the world of your story. Being confronted instead with a blank page (or screen) can feel daunting at times; it's often easier to begin a new scene when your writing muscles have already been warmed up.

> I write with a ballpoint pen on A4 sized narrow-lined paper. The paper has got to have a grey or blue margin and two holes. I only write on one side, and when I've got to the bottom of the last page, I finish the sentence (or write one more) at the top of the next, so that the paper I look at each morning isn't blank. It's already beaten.
>
> Philip Pullman

The writer's mind

Being a successful writer means making friends with your imagination. Writing isn't just about putting words on the page. Writers can be at work while taking a bath, going for a walk, cooking their tea. Any activity that allows your mind to wander freely – working out story ideas or problems, or simply drifting and wondering 'what if?' – can be part of writing.

Being receptive to this state of mind is important. Remember daydreaming, that pleasant activity that you got told off for in school? It's a writer's best friend. Just gazing out the window, letting your thoughts go where they will, is a meaningful activity when you're a writer. You never know where ideas will come from, but they are far more likely to arrive if you simply let your mind wander.

Sometimes, though, just hearing your own thoughts can be a challenge. We live in a society where we're constantly besieged by other people's messages: email, radio, television, and so on. Get into the habit of turning off this external chatter whenever you can. If you commute to work, try leaving your MP3 player at home, or not buying a newspaper. Just look out the window and see what's there. Or try leaving your headphones at home the next time you go to the gym, and let your mind drift as you work out.

A notebook is a vital tool for making friends with this deeper part of you. As you start listening to your imagination, you'll find it clamouring for your attention more and more. Wonderful ideas will come, and if you don't write them down, you may well forget them. I own many notebooks, all in different shapes and sizes, and take one with me wherever I go. I can't say this loudly enough: *Buy a notebook!* (And pardon me for shouting, but this is important!)

Your notebook doesn't need to be an expensive one. In fact, cheap ones with colourful plastic covers are often the best, as you don't feel obliged to fill them with great thoughts. A writer's notebook isn't about great thoughts. It's about capturing ideas as they fly past: scribbling descriptions of the passenger on the train opposite you; working out story problems; recording a quirky thought that might be a good idea for a novel. I always keep a notebook on my bedside table, too, so that I can jot down any interesting dreams I may have, or note story ideas that pop into my head at 4.00 am.

In short, your notebook is for anything you want to write in it. And although it may be filled with what would look like absolute rubbish to anyone else, that 'rubbish' is hugely important. Even if you only end up using a tiny portion of the material in your notebook, it's a vital seeding-ground where you can play and explore.

> I can't believe that everyone isn't having ideas all the time. I think they are, actually, and they just don't recognize them as potential stories. Because the important thing is not just having the idea; it's writing the book. That's the difficult thing, the thing that takes the time and the energy and the discipline. The initial idea is much less important than what you do with it.
>
> Philip Pullman

Establish links with other writers in your genre

Writing can be a lonely business, especially when you're first starting out. Establishing links with other writers in your genre can be a lifesaver. Apart from the pleasure of having others to talk with who share your concerns, hopes and frustrations, you can receive invaluable practical help: swap tips about submitting your work; provide each other with publishing contacts; read each other's work for comments.

Writers' groups are an excellent way to connect with other writers. You can find a list of UK writers' groups at www.nawg.co.uk, or else check with your local library or bookshop to see if they know of one operating in your area. Alternatively, start your own. When I first began writing, I put an advert for a writers' group in the local paper, and soon had a group that met weekly for several years. Online groups can also be extremely good, particularly if you live in a remote area and there aren't any other writers around. (See 'Taking it further' for a listing of some websites you might want to explore.)

While a generic writers' group is much better than nothing, the ideal is to find a group that writes the same type of fiction as you. Children's writing, for instance, has very different concerns to writing adult fantasy, and a mainstream thriller has very different concerns from chick-lit. While any writers' group will understand *some* of the issues you face, the only sort of group that will really understand exactly where you're coming from is one made up of authors from the same genre, so it's worth seeking out one of these (or starting your own).

You should also try to find a writers' group with a good mix of professional and non-professional writers. Online groups are especially good for this, though if you live in one of the larger cities, there might well be such a writers' group in your area. Be aware that some groups are better than others, so if you've found a group that isn't a good fit for you, then move on. There are others out there.

> I went to a very good writing class for quite a few years. The feedback from the other writers in the class (published and unpublished) was invaluable. Having others read your stories out loud rather than being allowed to read them aloud yourself was a real eye-opener. Others in the class would comment on characterization, plot structure, etc. whilst the writer was not allowed to speak until everyone had critiqued the work first.
>
> Malorie Blackman

Writing courses, especially residential ones, are another great way to forge links with other writers. Magazines such as *Mslexia* and *Writing* list many such courses each month. Residential courses are often genre-specific, or else you can look for one taught by an author who writes in your chosen genre. These courses aren't cheap, but they're usually very good value for the money. You'll meet other writers who you can then stay in touch with, and will also meet at least one professional – the tutor.

You might also consider going to a **writers' convention**. Most genres have their own central bodies, and hold annual conventions that both professionals and non-professionals can attend. Again, these aren't cheap, but they're well worth doing, as you'll meet a wealth of other writers who are just starting out, as well as professional authors, agents and publishers (and, in the case of the agents and publishers, they're often looking for new talent).

Whatever route you take, you'll find almost without exception that writing is a very friendly field. New writers tend to forge bonds easily with each other, and more established authors often greet newcomers with an honest willingness to help. Good contacts won't get you published, but they can certainly help to ease your way. Seek out other writers and make friends with them. The support you receive in return will be invaluable.

Writing buddies

Once you start meeting other writers, be on the lookout for a writing buddy or two; trusted writer-friends with whom you can swap your work, and then give feedback to each other. Having a writing buddy isn't mandatory – I know professional authors who have never shown their unpublished work to a single soul – but, just like having contacts, a good writing buddy can ease your way immensely. They'll spot problems in your story that you haven't noticed, help you sort sticky plot-points, and bounce ideas around with you. I'm lucky enough to have several writing-friends whose opinions I trust, and the feedback they've given me on early drafts of my books has saved me countless hours of heading down the wrong direction.

> It's much too easy to fall in love with your own prose. And dangerous. I have a few people I really trust, and if they tell me something's not working, I listen.
>
> Meg Rosoff

It's often good if writing buddies are at roughly the same stage in their writing careers, and if they write for the same or a similar genre. It's important that you're on the same wavelength, as your writing buddy needs to grasp exactly what you're trying to do with your writing, and vice versa. When they give you feedback on your work, you should instantly feel that they've understood your story perfectly. Their comments should resonate instinctively with you, and feel 'right' (even if a tiny part of you is miffed that they didn't think your story was a work of genius). You should feel similarly in tune with their work, so that when you read examples of it you can spot problem areas and have ideas about how to solve them.

Finding a good writing buddy often happens somewhat serendipitously once you begin to widen your field of contacts. Be on the lookout for them, and when you find a few, keep them close and treat them well. They are both your support and your safety net.

Don't talk too much

New writers are often brimming with excitement, eager to talk about what they're writing (at length and in great detail) to anyone who's willing to listen: that sympathetic stranger they've just met at the pub; a crowd of friends at a party; their co-workers; their mum. However, what these writers often find is that when they actually sit down to write, they no longer have enough enthusiasm left for their story to finish it: they've talked it out of their system. It's a generalization, but you can often spot new writers simply by the fact that they're so keen to tell you all about what they're writing.

In contrast, professional writers, as a rule, don't like to talk about works in progress until they have a complete draft in place – not because they're afraid of them being stolen (idea theft is actually pretty rare in the writing world), but because they know how easily story ideas can be destroyed by talking about them. And they also know the wonderful, compelling power that an idea can gain if you keep it close to your chest.

Stories demand an outlet, and if your outlet is other people, it's far less likely that your stories will make it onto paper. Story ideas are precious things – treat them preciously; don't bandy them about to anyone who'll listen. In fact, be downright mysterious when people ask about what you're writing. It drives other people mad, and adds a lovely frisson of secret enjoyment to your work.

Be in it for the long haul

In most cases, learning how to write publishable commercial fiction isn't something that can be picked up quickly, any more than playing the piano professionally. Talent helps a great deal, but becoming published also takes dedication and a substantial investment in time. In fact, I've heard it estimated that in terms of time spent learning and practising, becoming a published author is on a par with becoming a brain surgeon. While this sort of time scale won't be the case for everyone, it does give you an idea of the sort of commitment that's often needed.

So be in it for the long haul. Accept that it might take years for you to reach your dream; if you go into it with that mentality, you'll be far less likely to give up in frustration. Believe in yourself, believe in your stories, and keep writing. If you have talent and dedication, you're likely to succeed.

> My main advice is to get a cat. They're the best possible company while you're writing, and provide an excellent object lesson in how to cope when things aren't going well. Lie by the radiator, and go to sleep.
>
> Michael Marshall Smith

02

characterization

In this chapter you will learn:
- techniques for planning and creating characters
- how to select a viewpoint for your narrative
- about the different character types and their functions.

Your characters provide readers with the emotional key, the route into your story. You might have the most perfectly structured, brilliant plot on the planet, but if your characters are flat and lifeless, no one will want to read it.

There is a sort of magic that occurs when you've created a strong character, where he or she literally seems to come alive and starts doing things you didn't expect. This is an exhilarating feeling, part of the sheer joy of being a writer. And when you have a whole cast of strong characters in place, practically all you need to do is sit back and type – your characters will quite gladly take over and show you the way, with dialogue and actions seemingly appearing with no input from you.

But how do you make this magic happen? There are many concrete tips that I'll be sharing with you, but good characters can't be forced or 'invented' – it's more a matter of discovering who they are and getting to know them. Sometimes characters will come slowly, revealing themselves to you a facet at a time; sometimes they'll burst into being all at once.

Observe!

Writers tend to be avid people-watchers, endlessly fascinated by the things people do and say, and it's this constant study of other people that gives their characters depth and truth. So make people-watching your hobby. Observe the parade of humanity around you, and write down the tics and traits that catch your attention: the seventeen-year old girl who sucks her thumb when she thinks no one is looking; the man in the smart suit who squints his eyes almost shut as he reads; the overweight woman who talks so quickly that her words shove against each other like jostling shoppers.

However, don't be content with simply observing. Ask yourself questions about the people you see. Does that lady in the smart suit have a secret? How did that homeless man you pass every day end up sleeping on the street? Imagining stories about strangers isn't just a good way to flex your creative muscles; it will also help you find vivid characters and understand their motivations.

> I also watch people on the tube and write down notes. I've learned that if I don't write them down immediately, they vanish when I try to recall them.
>
> Jane Bidder

Try this

Gaze at someone you don't know for a few moments (take care they don't see you; the goal isn't to make them nervous), and then quickly write a few paragraphs describing them, in as much detail as you can: 'The bald man has eyes as dark as chocolate and wild, grizzled eyebrows; his cheeks are sallow, and his mouth thin as paper.' When you've captured a good word-picture of them, leave real life behind and move on to fiction. Ask yourself: 'What is his life like? What does he most fear? Where is he going now?' Delve deeply into this character, letting the ideas come to you as they will. Don't censor or judge; just write. Find out who the character is; what he wants; his frustrations and hopes. This is a brilliant exercise for practising characterization, and learning to trust your own instincts about who a character is.

Using real people as characters

Beware of using friends and family members as part of your cast – and not just for reasons of self-preservation. It's fine to use real people as starting points, but they should just be a rough model: broad character traits or physical descriptions. The ins and outs of your characters' psyches – their motivations, their hopes and dreams, their fears – need to come from you, so that you know exactly what's in their hearts. As you can never truly know this about someone else, you'll be held back in developing your character if you cling to what's actually 'real'.

Vital statistics

Though some writers prefer to find out about their characters as they write about them, I think it's extremely useful to do some basic planning about your cast before you plunge into writing. Your characters drive your plot, so if you know them well beforehand, you'll almost certainly find out all sorts of things that will affect your story arc. Ultimately, learning about your characters as a starting point can both save time and enrich your story.

First, decide on the basics. What does your character look like? You might 'see' him or her instantly in your mind, or you might need to experiment a bit to get an image that feels right to you. Height, build, age, complexion, hair and eye colour – these are all essential to know. Is she a 50-year-old tiny Asian woman with short black hair and snapping eyes? Is he 22, tall and thin, painfully pale with green eyes and thinning blonde hair?

Once you have the basic image, delve deeper. Perhaps he has a full, incongruous beard that he's proud of; perhaps she used to be a dancer and still keeps herself fit and toned. Pay attention also to how they move; how they speak; what sort of body language they use. Does she walk leisurely, taking her time, or rush about like a mad thing? Does he speak in a clear, booming voice, or mumble every word? All of these details tell us much more than simply how the character appears to others.

Then, ask yourself what sort of clothes he or she wears. Be specific about the little details; choice of clothing says a great deal about the type of person someone is. Does an aging businessman wear staid grey suits, but brighten them up with a flashy cartoon tie? Does a primary school teacher secretly wear lacy red lingerie under her proper teacher's clothes? Again, these are all details that help fix a character's personality, along with their appearance.

Your character's name is another vital aspect of their persona, and can subtly enhance or alter the image you've decided on. You might find that your character's name comes to you quite naturally as you sharpen your image of them in your mind, or else you might have to do some thinking about it, perhaps flipping through phonebooks or books of baby names for ideas. Your character's name should feel like a perfect 'summing up' of them. You'll know the right name when you find it.

When you've named your character and have their image sharply focused in your mind, write a detailed description of them, making it as vivid as possible (you'll use a lot of this detail when you start to write). Sometimes authors also find photos that look like their different characters, or if you're artistic you could try drawing them. Do whatever is useful for you so that you can see your characters clearly, and check in with your instincts as you go. Your character should be emerging to you, not invented by you.

> My characters tend to be quite vivid, arriving in my head fully-formed.
>
> Meg Rosoff

Getting to know them

Even if you didn't start out with an idea of what your character is like, you probably found yourself getting a sense of their personality as you worked out their physical appearance. Start to develop that now. Find out who your character is, and what makes him or her tick. The following exercises can be revelatory.

Key word exercise

Keeping the image of your character firmly in mind, write down one or two 'key words' that sum up what he or she is about. Don't think too deeply about these; again, trust your intuition. Is she artistic and generous? Great, write it down: 'Mandy Tomlin is artistic and generous.'

Next, still concentrating on your character, let some related words and phrases come into your mind that expand upon this theme: 'creative', 'kind', 'larger than life', 'flamboyant'. Some of your related words may go off in a slightly different direction from your key words; that's fine. Write down your related words as a list underneath your defining sentence, and keep going until you have at least ten words apart from your key words.

Now, go back to your key words and add some opposing traits. If you've written 'She is artistic and generous', add the word 'but …' and see what comes. You might get something like, 'She is artistic and generous, but hates compliments and bristles when she receives one.' Continue the exercise using pairs of your related words: 'She is creative and flamboyant, but is extremely punctual. She is dramatic and kind, but doesn't suffer fools gladly.' Play around with pairing different combinations, and see what various opposing traits you get.

Finally, delve deeper. Look for explanations. Going back to your key words, add the word 'Why?' to them. 'She is artistic and generous.' Why? 'Because she was raised by her adoring grandparents, who encouraged her talent and taught her that life is about giving.' You might find yourself expanding on these sentences and writing more at this stage, as pieces of your character's past and personality fall into place: 'They spoiled her a bit, but they couldn't help themselves; they felt so sorry for her for being an orphan.' Go with it; write as much as you want to, playing with different word pairs from your list of related words. Search for explanations of your opposing traits, too: 'She is creative and flamboyant, but is extremely punctual because she can't bear the thought of missing out on anything.'

At the end of this exercise, you might be amazed at all that you've found out: in-depth pieces of your character's past; insights into their hopes and fears; detailed information about their relationships with others. At the very least, you should have a well-rounded idea of who your character is and why they act the way they do. I find this exercise particularly useful because it leads you away from two-dimensional thinking, where you simply have 'good' or 'bad' characters. It's also extremely flexible, and can be modified to explore any aspect of your character you like: mannerisms, fears, family history, and so on.

Change voice

If you write in the third person, another good exercise is to write about a character in the first person for a few pages. Get right into their head and let them speak for themselves; you might be surprised at what they say to you. Or, if you normally write in the first person, try writing about your character in the third, letting the 'camera' of the narrative observe their actions and expressions.

Character questionnaire

Finally, you can write an extensive 'character questionnaire', personalizing it for your genre. This should be as comprehensive as possible, covering everything about your character you can think of: physical appearance, mannerisms, background, family relationships (these in particular can give you vital insight into motivation), present situation, and so on. What does your character do for a living? What is their greatest secret, their biggest fear? What do they have in their closet? Pretend that you're a spy who has been hired to find out absolutely everything about this character, and write your questionnaire accordingly. Save a template on computer if possible, so that you can use it again for other characters. The information you discover through answering these questions may amaze you.

These exercises are the best tools I know for taking you deeply into a character – from the external appearance to different character traits to the reasons behind them. The possible revelations (along with possible stories) are endless. Remember that even if some of the information you discover doesn't have a place in the story (and not all of it will), it's still vital for you as the author to know it. The goal is to know your characters so well that you know instantly how they might act in any situation.

CHARACTER QUESTIONNAIRE

CHARACTER'S FULL NAME:
Reason or meaning of name:

Nickname:	Reason for nickname:
Birth date:	Astrological sign:

PHYSICAL APPEARANCE:

Age:	How old does s/he appear?
Eye colour:	Glasses or contacts?

Weight:	Height:	Type of body/build:
Skin tone:	Skin type:	Shape of face:

Distinguishing marks:

Predominant feature:

Hair colour, type (coarse, fine, thick) and typical hairstyle:

Looks like:

Is s/he healthy?	If not, why not:

Physical disabilities, if any:

ATTITUDE:

Daredevil or cautious?	Same when alone?
Character's greatest fear:	Why?

What is the worst thing that could happen to him/her?

What single event would most throw character's life into complete turmoil?

Character is most at ease when:

Most ill at ease when:

Priorities:

Philosophy of life, if any:

How s/he feels about self:

Past failure s/he would be embarrassed to have people know about:

If granted one wish, what would it be?

CURRENT SITUATION:

Job/profession:

Are they doing what they most want to do?

If not, what would they rather be doing?

Where does character live?

Where does character want to live?

Does character have a significant other?	What is the relationship like if so?
Children?	Names, how many, what are the relationships with them like?

What sort of car do they drive?

What sort of house do they live in?

What are the character's finances like?

BACKGROUND:

Home town:

What was early childhood like?

First memory:

Most important early childhood event that still affects him/her:

Religion, if any:

Finances:

FAMILY:

Mother:	Relationship with her:
Father:	Relationship with him:
Siblings:	Birth order:
Relationship with each sibling:	Children of siblings, if any:
Extended family?	Close? Why or why not?

One of the titbits I picked up from a sitcom writing course was to do a full profile for each of your characters so that you get to know them really well. That's how I now start the process of setting a novel out. I spend a couple of weeks writing extensive background information for each character – which I hardly ever use in the story – and picking out photographs from glossy mags of people who they might look like. As I start my novel I keep that to hand for the first few chapters until I feel I'm well acquainted with them. I feel that if you know your characters well then you don't have to shoe-horn them into situations. As the plot develops you know instinctively how your character would react.

Carole Matthews

Describing your characters

You should by now have an in-depth idea of exactly what your characters look like, and how they appear both to themselves and others. The key in using this information effectively in your writing is to not overwhelm readers with masses of description all at once. The first time a character makes an appearance in your story, give your readers a quick idea of what he or she looks like, and then provide further details as the story continues.

For instance, the first time we meet a character you might have something like the following:

James gripped her hand, his palm rough against hers. His eyes were charcoal, and the harsh lines on either side of his mouth made his face look carved in wood. He wore faded jeans and carried a spade, and when Sally withdrew her hand, he leaned on its worn wooden handle, regarding her silently.

Then, a few lines later, you might sneak in a bit more description:

Smudges of pure silver daubed James's temples. Unexpectedly, he smiled, showing a gold front tooth. 'Aye, you might think that.' His accent was pure Geordie, and Sally wondered what he was doing so far south.

Once you have a character firmly described, it's a good idea to 'remind' readers of what they look like occasionally, so that they can see your characters vividly. Inserting action and description around bits of dialogue is especially good for this:

> *He jabbed the spade into the earth and shot her a dark-eyed glance. 'You don't know what you're asking, pet,' he said.*

Don't slow your narrative down with masses of detail, but do give readers specific images that they can see, so that your scenes and characters jump into life.

Viewpoint

Should you write your story in the first person, or the third? First person is the 'I' voice, where your main character tells the story in his or her own words; third person refers to the main character as 'he' or 'she'. Ultimately, the choice will come down to what feels most natural to you. Both voices have pros and cons.

Some authors find the **first-person voice** much easier than third, and it certainly has its advantages. The primary one is that you're directly in the main character's mind, which gives the reader instant access to everything they're thinking and feeling. If done well, this can result in a lovely feeling of intimacy and freshness. The first-person voice does have limitations, though: if you're writing in the 'I' voice, you can't suddenly dip into a different character's head and let the reader know what's going on there; neither can you show the reader anything that the main character can't see, or inform them of things they don't know.

While the **third-person voice** might lack the immediate intimacy of the first person, you do have the option of moving the narrative camera back slightly, and viewing your character from the outside as well as from within. In the third-person voice you also have the freedom to leave your main character and describe a scene that they have no knowledge of, which can be an extremely useful device for heightening tension and revealing needed exposition. (Effective ways of handling both third- and first-person voice are discussed in Chapter 06, under 'Get inside your main character's head'.)

Try this

Using the first person, write about a character who's just had a dark secret discovered. Your 'I' voice can be either the person who's just been rumbled, or the one who's found the secret out – whichever feels most dramatic to you. Write for a few pages, getting into the character's voice and letting them tell the story of what happened. Then, write the same story from the third person point of view. Which do you find easier? Which feels more natural to you?

Should you have **varying viewpoints**, where your story is told from the perspective of more than one person, switching back and forth between them? Varying viewpoints can add an interesting slant to a story, though in epic dramas with a large cast you should be sure that every character is really needed. You should also take care that you *never have more than one viewpoint per scene*. As we'll be discussing in depth in the next chapter, scenes need to have a central point of tension, and this is difficult to achieve if you're dipping about in different characters' heads – not to mention that doing so can feel sloppy and unclear.

Your main character

Your main character is the viewpoint character of your story: the 'I' voice in a first-person narrative, or the character whose thoughts and actions are followed in a third-person narrative. Also known as your **protagonist or hero**, your main character may well be the single most important element of your story. He or she provides the emotional key; they're the means through which readers experience your world.

Readers should 'click' with him or her right from the first page, and be rooting for them to succeed on through to the end. In the current best-seller *The Undomestic Goddess,* author Sophie Kinsella accomplishes this character hook very neatly. She shows us her workaholic main character Samantha attempting to relax on a spa pamper-day, but being unable to, sneaking in her BlackBerry and mobile phone. By the end of this short opening chapter, we like Sam; we can empathize with her hectic lifestyle, and we can see, even if she can't, how desperately she needs to slow down. And, by the time we get to the main action, where Samantha loses her job, we are completely on her side.

This is what you're aiming for. Main characters don't have to be people you'd like in real life – Samantha would undoubtedly be irritatingly work-obsessed if one were to actually meet her – but readers do need to understand where your main character is coming from, and to enjoy his or her company. A story is a journey. If your readers dislike their guide, they're unlikely to finish the trip.

> I've had to turn down novels where there has been a great story, very well written, but the characters and their attitudes are so repugnant that I couldn't imagine anyone wanting to spend 300 pages in their company.
>
> Annette Green, Annette Green Authors' Agency

However, just as in real life, not all readers are going to like all main characters, and that's perfectly fine. The important thing is not to err on the side of caution, or else you'll run the risk of having a bland, boring main character that no one at all can connect with. Instead, make sure that *you* find your main character utterly fascinating and involving. Don't be afraid to be bold, or bigger than life. Think about some of the main characters who have stayed with us through time: Scarlett O'Hara, Holden Caulfield, Sherlock Holmes. While these characters all feel complex and real, they're also painted in deliciously broad strokes; the authors weren't timid about creating big, memorable main characters. Neither should you be. Agents and publishers see a lot of dull protagonists; make yours stand out.

You should also make sure that your main character's age and sex are appropriate to your genre. While some types of fiction have more leeway here than others, genres such as children's fiction, romance, and chick-lit often have certain expectations attached to them, and you'll improve your chances if you're aware of these. If you do break the rules it should be a choice made from an informed understanding of your genre, rather than a blunder made out of ignorance.

It's an author's job to know all of his characters well, but you should in particular know your main character. Use the exercises described previously, until he or she is a real person to you and you know instantly how they would react in any given situation – what they would say; how they would feel.

A reader's knowledge of a main character comes through you, and if you as the author don't feel that you know your main character well, then your readers haven't got a chance.

If you choose to write a story with varying viewpoints you might be developing several main characters, and this can be a very effective device: Marian Keyes's best-selling *The Other Side of the Story* comes to mind as an example, along with many of Terry Pratchett's best-sellers. However, be sure that each of your heroes has a vital slant on the overall story to tell, and that you're not just switching voices for the sake of it.

The villain

The villain, or **antagonist,** is the character whom your main character is struggling against, such as Sherlock Holmes's nemesis Moriarty. Not all books have villains, and the idea of a villain as pure evil is a somewhat outdated concept nowadays, particularly in real-life genres. (Over-the-top evil villains still appear regularly in children's fantasy, however.) If you choose to have a villain, have fun with them, and let them be a bit bigger than life, such as Fagin in *Oliver Twist* – readers love to hate a really good villain.

However, don't let them be two-dimensional. Use the exercises described and know where they're coming from, and how they've ended up the way they have. Though they're thwarting your main character, you as the author should still have understanding for your villain. The horrific Professor Umbridge in *Harry Potter and the Order of the Phoenix* is a good example here. She's a hugely effective villain, precisely because she's been thought through in such consistent, in-depth detail by J. K. Rowling. And, though readers gasp in delighted horror at Umbridge, I'd be surprised if Rowling herself hated her – it's impossible to despise characters whom you understand so well.

In fact, sometimes authors find that they have more fun with their villains than with their main characters. Be sure that you keep the balance right, and remember to make your main character fascinating in his or her own right. Your villain shouldn't steal their thunder; at the end of the day, your readers should want the hero to prevail.

Secondary and minor characters

Secondary characters are important characters who aren't your protagonist, such as Mammy in *Gone with the Wind*, and Ron Weasley in *Harry Potter*. While they aren't usually viewpoint characters, they're still vital cast members, and their actions and concerns will influence the direction that the story will take. Try the exercises described previously for them. You may not choose to go into quite as much depth as for your main character, but do spend some time getting to know your secondary characters. You should know where they're coming from: what motivates them, and why.

Minor characters are characters who may only have a single appearance in your story. It's not necessary to know their lives in detail, but you still want them to jump into life as a vivid snapshot. I find astrological signs, with their broad descriptions of character traits, very useful for the rapid sketching of minor characters. (You might want to invest in a cheap guide to the different star signs; it's a handy reference to have in your writer's library.) A shop clerk might be a 'cheerful Virgo', or the waitress an 'affronted Leo'. Naturally, this isn't information that the reader will know, but it's useful for you as the author, just to have an easy grasp on who the character is and what mood they're in. This technique will help add depth and truth to even the most minor of appearances.

What's the problem?

Keep in mind that your main character must have a definite **problem** that he or she is trying to overcome, and that their attempts to solve this problem will form the structure of your story. This is the fundamental basis of what a story is: a main character who is striving against the odds to obtain some sort of goal. Without a crucial problem facing your main character, there's quite simply no story.

As you work through the various exercises in this chapter, see if you can discover what your main character's problem is. Types of problem will of course vary greatly depending upon genre, but whether it's saving the world or finding true love, your hero must care deeply about the result. The problem should also be **personal** to your main character: he or she must be emotionally involved; the one who has the most to gain or lose by the outcome.

'Saving the world' is too abstract for most of us to really take on board, but add the personal element of a hero whose family is being held hostage by the villain, and readers will be on the edge of their seats.

Try this

Write down ten novels that you've read. Now, write down the overall problem that faces the main character(s) in each one. With some novels this will be more obvious than others, but the problem will always be there. If you can't think of one for a particular novel, reread it. You might be surprised to find that there's a problem so subtly woven into the story that it's not what stuck in your mind, but it's there all the same – driving the story forward, and acting as scaffolding holding it together.

Emotional journey

Your characters need to be real people, affected by the events they're going through, so that when the story ends some sort of emotional shift has occurred: perhaps they've overcome a fear, or become less naïve, or learned to trust. This is known as a character's **emotional journey**, and is vital to creating gripping fiction. However, don't try to force the details of a character's emotional journey – the issues they face should arise naturally from your knowledge of their background and personalities. As you get to know them, it should become obvious to you where they have room to grow and change. Let your characters show you the way here.

While it's particularly important for your main character to have an emotional journey, other important characters need to have one, too. In Stephen King's epic blockbuster *The Stand,* the characters are all richly drawn, and undergo significant changes as the story goes on. Stu goes from being a shy loner to the confident leader of a colony; Larry goes from being a self-obsessed rock star to sacrificing himself for his friends. Without this sense of real characters undergoing real shifts and changes, your story isn't as likely to grab readers' hearts and minds and make them care about your work. (If your story isn't about something important enough to change your characters' lives in some way, then you need to rethink it.)

However, don't let it happen all at once, for example with the evil villain unexpectedly seeing the light at the end and atoning for his sins. Just as in real life, events throughout the story should transform your characters step by step, so that any change by the end feels inevitable and true.

How many?

An over-large cast isn't an advantage; a long parade of names can easily become confusing for a reader, not to mention that if you're trying to juggle a cast of 30 characters, then some of them are bound to feel skimpy and incomplete. As a general rule, it's stronger to have fewer characters who can then be more fully developed. Just as in real life, it's difficult to be intimate with strangers. Readers need time to feel that they know a particular character, and this is unlikely to happen if your novel is more like a heaving nightclub than an intimate party.

So don't add new characters just because you can; make sure that they're really needed. *The only reason to have a character in place is that he or she fulfils a role that no other character can fulfil.* When you're planning your story, you should have an idea of the function that every character will be playing in it. If you have lots of characters who each perform only a minor function, then ask yourself whether you can merge a few of them, or cut some of them out altogether. Having fewer characters will allow the ones left to take on a stronger, more three-dimensional role, making it easier for readers to connect to them.

Honesty has to be key. You have to ask yourself questions like, 'Do I really need that character?' 'Does that scene work?' 'Would that person really behave like this?' And you have to give honest answers and be prepared to cut out extraneous material and fun, but functionless, characters.

Barbara Nadel

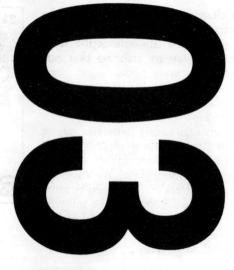

03

plot and scene structure

In this chapter you will learn:
- how to consider the structure of your overall narrative
- how to plan the structure of individual scenes and the movement between them
- the value of setting and research when planning narrative structure.

So you've got a great main character, you know what their problem is … now what? Unfortunately, it's not enough to have wonderful characters and a compelling problem. Stories also demand a strong inner logic: a step-by-step ordering of events that makes sense and feels satisfying to a reader. Agents and publishers see near misses every day that lack a clear form. Structure is about knowing where you're going, and it's an essential skill for blockbuster fiction.

> If a script is extremely well written that doesn't clinch it on its own – there has to be a compelling story and engaging characters. To me these remain the three pillars of storytelling in a novel (and mostly in non-fiction as well). I've turned down novels where the writing was spell-binding, but so little happened that the narrative never even got started.
>
> Annette Green, Annette Green Authors' Agency

Plot structure

Structure, like discipline, sounds like something of a dirty word – a necessary evil, a duty rather than a pleasure. It sounds, in fact, like the complete opposite of fun, spontaneous creativity. Yet plot and scene structure are the unsung heroes of good writing, the underlying support system that will allow the rest of your story to fly. Without a solid structure in place, characters and story incidents often drift about aimlessly, wandering down unneeded side-trails and spouting irrelevant dialogue. Think of your favourite book or favourite film. Almost certainly, it has a strong underlying structure in place, pulling the story together into a clear, logical form.

Good story structure, like many elements of good writing, has the invisibility factor: when it's done well, you don't even notice it. We all know *lack* of story structure when we hear it – just think of the office bore, droning on ad nauseam about their pointless activities until you want to scream. Our knowledge of structure is largely instinctive. We know when a story feels strong and solid, and we know when it feels meandering and pointless. It's just a matter of taking it apart and understanding what's at work under the surface, so that you can then begin to apply it to your own writing.

> The most difficult thing I had to learn was how to construct a story. Oral storytelling helped me there – it gives you a feel for pace – but I still think it's the hardest thing to do, especially since I never work out plots in advance – I just have a rough idea of where I'm headed, and then start. This means the story often develops in ways I never expected. But it can be torture working it out, because it still has to have a satisfactory shape.
>
> Katherine Langrish

The three-act structure

The three-act structure is a contemporary interpretation of plot, and is the most commonly used model of dramatic structure in both film and commercial fiction. Even if you've never encountered this concept before, it will very likely seem familiar to you, as this is the structure behind most of your favourite novels, films and childhood fairytales. A good understanding of it can enhance your writing considerably, by giving your stories a cohesive shape and form.

Act 1: set-up

Act 1 is the story's beginning, or **set-up**. This is where you introduce the reader to your main character(s) and your world (time, setting, genre), along with the current status quo: what life is like for your characters, and why the reader should care about them. Making sure that readers connect with your main character from the start is crucial.

Act 1 is usually quite brief: only a few pages or a single chapter. For real-life genres in particular, you normally won't need a great deal of time to get across what life is like for your characters, though for genres such as fantasy and sci-fi, where you might be introducing a whole new world, the set-up could take quite a bit longer.

In the best-selling *Girl With a Pearl Earring* by Tracy Chevalier, the set-up is only a few pages long. Griet, the main character, is in her mother's kitchen when an important stranger and his wife arrive to meet her. We can tell that Griet is nervous, and we sympathize, as it becomes clear that this lavish pair are considering having her work for them, and that she has mixed feelings about this. As the scene goes on, the man – who is the painter Vermeer – notices the way Griet has been chopping the vegetables for the family meal, with each vegetable carefully arranged according to colour. When he questions her about this, he and the reader receive further insight into Griet: she is artistic, and being a maid is probably not what she dreams of for herself.

By the end of the scene, where Griet's mother tells her that she has no choice but to be the Vermeers' maid, we are in full sympathy with the girl, and by the time we get to the story's action, where Griet starts work at Vermeer's house, we are firmly on her side: we wish things could be better for her, and are interested in her as a character. Though only a few pages long, the set-up here is crucial. It shows the reader who Griet is and what motivates her, and also hints at the turbulent relationships to come between herself, Vermeer, and Vermeer's wife.

At the end of the set-up comes the **inciting event,** or **first plot point**: the event that propels the main character from their normal life into some sort of problem that must be solved. In *Girl With a Pearl Earring*, this occurs when Griet's mother tells her that she must take the job with the Vermeers. Stories often begin very close to this first plot point, and fill in any needed information about the main character's previous life as the story progresses. Keeping close to the action and keeping the story moving forward are key.

Act 2: conflict

The inciting event springboards us into the second act, or the **conflict**. Act 2 will comprise the bulk of your story, where your main character attempts to overcome the central problem (which may shift or change focus as the story goes on).

This middle section of your story is all about rising tension. Your main character is attempting to overcome the central problem, but despite (or because of) her efforts, the situation grows tenser and tenser, with mounting obstacles and complications along the way. Each complication leads to a minor climax, building in power from the last, and so on up to your story's ultimate climax.

In the graph on the next page, note how the story arc is an unbroken line, rather than a series of unconnected dots. That line represents your overall plot, and shows that your story's events need to be *linked* to each other with **cause and effect**, with each

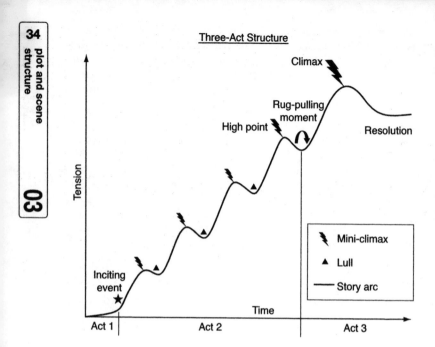

Three-Act Structure

plot turn dependent upon the last. This is a crucial point. In real life, events are random, but fiction demands internal logic and structure: this happened *because* this happened.

After each mini-climax, there's a brief period of falling action, though the story's overall tension keeps rising. These little lulls are important, because they give your readers time to catch their breath, take in what has happened, and anticipate what's going to come. (We'll cover the art of pacing more thoroughly in Chapter 08.)

It's fine to have several story threads going at once, but the same rule applies: each individual story arc needs to be crafted with rising tension and cause and effect in mind, and eventually your different story threads should come together into a coherent ending. Keep things tight; keep things logical.

The **emotional journey** should also have a definite beginning, middle and end, with climaxes and lulls mirroring of the action structure. Both elements are vital, dancing together side by side up to an ultimate dual climax and resolution, as shown in the graph on the next page.

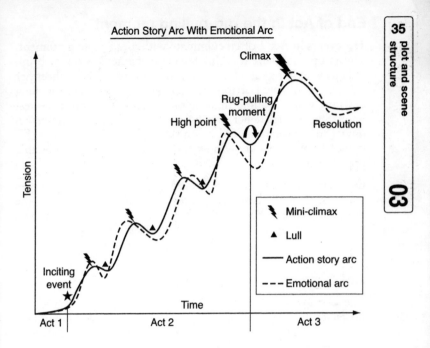

Action Story Arc With Emotional Arc

For instance, let's look at Margaret Mitchell's *Gone With the Wind*, one of the best-selling novels of all time. Much of the action storyline is about Scarlett O'Hara's attempts to hold on to Tara and survive during and in the aftermath of the American Civil War. That's the external (or action) problem, and it gives an urgency and a framework to the emotional storyline, which focuses on Scarlett's love of Ashley Wilkes, her relationship with Rhett Butler, and her gradual inner hardening as a result of her struggle to survive.

The action storyline is about *what* happens – the physical events relating to a specific overall problem – and this gives you the structure through which you can explore *how* it affects your main character: the emotional journey. If *Gone With the Wind* had simply been about Scarlett longing for a man she couldn't have, it would not have been the massive success it was. Similarly, it wouldn't have been anywhere near as gripping if Mitchell had simply written about Scarlett's struggle to survive without giving us any understanding of her hopes and dreams.

End of Act 2: the rug-pulling moment

The events in Act 2 often culminate with a **rug-pulling moment**. This is a point where we think the main character is on the brink of achieving her goal – but then, just as we're ready to cheer her triumph, it all goes horribly and unexpectedly wrong, propelling her into worse trouble than before. This is the hero's darkest hour. She has tried her hardest, but she cannot possibly win now. (Your readers should be on the edges of their seats at this point, desperate to know how the main character can possibly prevail after *that*.)

But all is not lost. If your story events have been properly woven together, then all the puzzle pieces should be in place once the dust has settled. Your main character will quickly put them together to realize or discover what needs to be done in order to succeed, and we enter the final stage of the story.

Act 3: climax and resolution

The **climax** is the culmination of all the complications and obstacles that have come before. This is the crisis point: the most involving moment in your story, where the main character struggles against the ultimate difficulty. Tension is at its peak. This is often the only chance that your hero has left, the all or nothing moment, where the stakes are at their absolute highest. If the main character doesn't succeed now, he never will – and he must *succeed or fail on his own merits*.

That last point is vital for an effective climax. Resist the urge to have the army abseil down the sides of the building, saving the day, or for another character to rush up out of nowhere, waving the previously undiscovered will that solves everything. Think of the novel *Silence of the Lambs,* and that gripping climax where Clarice is on her own in the building, looking for the kidnapped girl. Remember the moment when the lights go off – and although the villain has infra-red goggles, Clarice does not? The last thing that would have worked at that moment would have been if a SWAT team had burst in to save the day – the whole story would have fallen to pieces. Your hero should be the star, and when it comes to crunch time, she needs to resolve the problem on her own.

Whenever possible, it's desirable to have some sort of **plot twist** occur within your climax: something that's completely logical given the events that have come before, but that's also unexpected. Ideally, you want your readers to think, 'I never saw *that* coming – but it makes perfect sense.' This isn't always easy to accomplish, but is well worth striving for; books where readers can guess the outcome long before it occurs aren't anywhere near as gripping as those that keep them on their toes right to the very end. However, do make sure that any plot twists that occur are logical, natural outcomes of your story – don't try to trick your readers by withholding vital information or deceiving them.

Whether your climax should have a happy outcome or not depends upon genre and your own personal preference. Happy endings aren't mandatory, though they are expected in some genres, such as chick-lit and romantic fiction. In most genres, there's leeway for whatever you choose here, though you should keep in mind that endings that are absolute downers (where the plan fails and everyone dies, for instance) are usually avoided in commercial fiction, and for good reason. When someone invests their time in reading a novel, they want some sort of emotional payoff at the end. If you end without even a ray of hope readers are likely to feel irritated, and might wish they hadn't bothered with your story.

However, you often have outcomes that aren't clearly happy or sad, but are instead a mix of strong emotions. Looking at *Gone With the Wind* again, Scarlett learns of her deep love for Rhett just at the moment when Rhett decides to leave her. Scarlett has found her soul mate, but it might be too late; perhaps Rhett will never come back. Mitchell's genius in leaving this plot point unresolved is what helped make this novel such a blockbuster. A bittersweet twist at the end can add the sort of resonance that makes a story linger long in a reader's mind.

Regardless of whether your outcome is happy or not, the climax is the point from which the main characters cannot return: their lives have been irrevocably changed, and they must forge new lives for themselves from this point onwards. In general, the best endings are also new beginnings.

After the climax comes the **resolution**: the final 'lull', where loose ends are tied up and we see how the climax has affected the main character. How has he grown and changed from having gone through the events of the story? What has it all been about? This is where your reader will stop and take stock, and where you'll give them a final note that sets the mood upon which they'll finish your novel. Don't linger here for too long, though; nobody likes a guest who overstays his welcome. Just tell us what we need to know to feel satisfied from the story, and then take your leave.

Often stories will resolve some plot elements while leaving other questions open. This can be an effective device, but make sure that your emotional storyline reaches fulfilment, even if the action storyline does not. A good example is the hit children's novel *The Story of Tracy Beaker,* by Jacqueline Wilson. Tracy, a difficult young girl in care, longs to find a foster parent. At the story's end, although the answer to this central question remains unresolved, we close with the knowledge that Tracy has become, at least for the moment, a more understanding person.

Readers need to feel a sense of emotional roundedness and completion at the end of a story, and this sense will come through your main character having reached a new understanding or some sort of growth or change. However, if you choose to use this device, you must make sure that it's a calculated choice. *You* should know exactly how the action events pan out regardless of whether or not you decide to spell them out to your reader; the decision not to do so should never be made because you don't actually know what happens.

Anatomy of a blockbuster

Let's look at J. K. Rowling's ultra-blockbuster *Harry Potter and the Philosopher's Stone* as an example of how all of this works.

Act 1: set-up:

The **set-up** in this novel is fairly lengthy, as this is the start of an epic fantasy and the world and characters must be introduced. We learn about the secret world of wizards, the murder of Harry's parents by Voldemort, and his miserable life with the Dursleys. The status quo is well established by the time the **inciting event** (or **first plot point**) occurs about 30 pages in, with the arrival of Hagrid. We then move on to the second act: Harry at Hogwart's.

Act 2: conflict:

Here again, Rowling spends a lot of time setting up her world, with details about Harry's new friends and his life at school. You could argue that Rowling actually establishes a new status quo once Harry gets to Hogwart's, and that there is then a second inciting event about 100 pages in, when news of the break-in at Gringotts Bank is reported, and Harry realizes that the thieves must have been after whatever Hagrid had taken out earlier that day. In general, you don't want to wait this long to introduce your action plot. Rowling gets away with it through the sheer charm and invention of her concept, but most of us shouldn't count on that, so make sure your action plot appears as quickly as possible.

Once we reach this point, the action storyline starts to move at a much faster pace. Harry and his friends encounter the vicious three-headed dog on page 119, and quickly deduce that it must be guarding something – perhaps the object that Hagrid took from Gringotts. Harry then discovers Professor Snape with bite wounds on his leg, and realizes that Snape must have tried to steal whatever the three-headed dog is guarding. Shortly afterwards, Snape appears to try to jinx Harry as he plays in his first Quidditch match. The stakes are raised; is Snape trying to kill Harry? And so on, throughout the remainder of Act 2: events are linked to each other through **cause and effect**, with mini-climaxes and lulls as the overall tension rises.

A mystery that began as childish high spirits takes an ominous turn with the discovery that it is the philosopher's stone that has been hidden, and that Voldemort, who killed Harry's parents, is trying to get it, perhaps in league with Snape. The stakes have now skyrocketed. It is vital that the evil Voldemort is stopped, and given Harry's past, it is a problem that he cares passionately about, adding greatly to our own emotional involvement (emotional storyline working alongside the action storyline).

Harry's darkest hour (the **rug-pulling moment**, or **second plot point**, ending Act 2) comes with the realization that Dumbledore is not at Hogwart's and cannot help him: he must attempt to stop Voldemort on his own. Events have been inexorably set in motion, and everything is now in place for the story's climax.

Act 3: climax and resolution:

In Act 3, Harry and his friends manage to get past the series of traps protecting the stone, leading us to the **climax** between Harry and Voldemort – with the great twist that it wasn't Snape at all who was helping Voldemort, but the timorous Professor Quirrell. In a nail-gripping showdown, Harry manages to defeat them against all odds.

All that is then left is the **resolution**, where Harry wakes up in the infirmary and Dumbledore ties up the loose ends of the plot for us – and verifies that Voldemort is still out there somewhere. Harry has defeated him, but only for the moment. Yet we reach a satisfying emotional roundness when Gryffindor wins the House Cup, and end on a humorous note when Harry realizes that with the threat of magic hanging over them, the Dursleys will be too terrified to make his life miserable that summer.

> **Try this**
>
> Reread a favourite book, and see how it fits into the three-act structure. Is there a definite set-up? How is the mid-section structured? Is there a rug-pulling moment? Get in the habit of viewing stories structurally: see what points most have in common, and where some of them differ.

A word of caution

You should be familiar with the basics of plot structure, but you should also feel perfectly free to break its rules, so long as it's a conscious decision and you know why you're doing so. The three-act structure is a marvellous tool, but don't become a slave to it. It might be that one or two aspects of it aren't right for a particular story, or that you choose to mix up a few of its elements. That's fine. Follow your instincts, but do so from an informed position.

> Plot structure comes partly from experience and partly from the fact that a writer simply MUST read if he/she is ever going to amount to much. By which I don't mean you can copy someone's plotting, but you can learn from the way the 'greats' handle plot. I think experience shows you what is right for you and what you can and can't do.
>
> Katie Flynn

Scene structure

A scene is a sequence where a character or characters engage in some sort of action and/or dialogue. Scenes should have a beginning, middle and end (a mini-story arc), and should focus around a definite **point of tension** that moves the story forward. Scenes are the building blocks of story. No matter how well constructed your story ideas are, if your scenes aren't also properly constructed, it could all fall flat.

Tension is vital in a scene; it's what drama is all about. If everything is going exactly to plan and all your characters are happy, then there's usually no reason to have a scene. Tension doesn't have to mean that your characters are arguing, by the way, although it can mean that. It simply means that something isn't right; one or more of your characters is experiencing a negative emotion. This is often in relation to or in tandem with some sort of action that's relevant to the story.

Think of a scene as a simplified story arc, with a beginning, middle and end. The beginning of the scene sets the time and place, and as in the story's set-up, you want to keep this brief. The scene's mid-section moves along logically, building to some sort of definite point of tension. At the scene's end, this point has been resolved in some way. Though the larger story question has been left open, events have moved forward because of the events in the scene. And, once the central point of tension has been resolved, you end the scene as soon as possible, on a nicely rounded note.

Keep in mind that there are only two reasons to have a scene: either to **move the story forward**, or to give your reader **needed character information**. Ideally, a scene will accomplish both. Just as with your overall storyline, a scene shouldn't be about *only* action or *only* character – both are essential. So layer your scenes whenever possible; make them work for their keep. For instance, if you have one scene where two characters are having a conversation, and another scene where they're travelling to a new location, try merging them.

As an example of how all of this can work, here's a short scene from my second book, *Missing Abby* – a teenage novel which was shortlisted for the Edgar Allan Poe award in the US. The main character in the scene is thirteen-year-old Emma, who after a bad experience has changed schools and created a new persona for herself. She calls herself 'Ems' now, and wants to forget the voice of the bully from her past:

> *The bottom of my wardrobe was a complete tip, with heaps of old clothes and games shoved into it like a jumble sale. Dressed in the oversized blue T-shirt I wear to bed, I crouched on the floor and started pulling things out – an old scarf, a stuffed walrus called Simpson, a pair of boots.*

> *The box was still there, nestled in the very back of the wardrobe. I sat back on my heels, staring at it. It felt like some ancient archaeological relic, so in a way I was surprised that it hadn't collapsed into dust.*

I started to drag it out, and then stopped. Nothing had changed, really, had it? I was still Ems. And what was in the box had absolutely nothing to do with me any more. The carpet prickled against my bare knees as I crouched there, running my fingers over the cardboard lid.

'Isn't that sweet! Freaky is writing a story! Hey, everyone, listen to this – '"The two novice mages" – Oy! Quit trying to grab, you rude cow!'

My stomach lurched like I had just drunk a pint of rancid milk. I slammed the box back into place and went to bed.

Note the elements in place here. The first paragraph quickly sketches the time and place for us as we move to the action: Emma digs deeply into her wardrobe and takes out a box that's obviously important to her. The point of tension around which the scene revolves is, will she open the box? But difficult memories overwhelm Emma, and no, she does not: she shoves the box back into her wardrobe. The point of tension is therefore resolved for now, while the overall story has been moved forward: we are now aware that the box exists, and that it holds some sort of key to her past. The scene then ends on a 'round' note which completes it, so that we're not left hanging with this realization: Emma puts the box away and goes to bed. And, in terms of character, we are in Emma's head and privy to her feelings of confusion and fear, which add to the scene; we also get a glimpse in flashback of the bully character from her old school.

As this is teenage fiction, the writing might feel somewhat sparser than you're used to if you write in a wordier genre. However, even in longer or more complex scenes, the same rules apply: a central point of tension is needed, and the scene should have an ultimate purpose that's being accomplished in relation to the overall story. Before you begin to write a scene, it's a good idea to stop and work out exactly what this purpose is. What are you trying to do with the scene? Know your point of tension before you start to write, and structure your scene around it.

A good rule of thumb with scenes is to *get in late, get out early*. If you're writing a scene about a man who's decided to tell his wife that the marriage is over, don't start it with him waking up, brushing his teeth, taking out the rubbish, and so on. Start where the **action** is – as near to the actual point of conflict as possible. And, when you've accomplished what you wanted to with the scene, don't hang about: end it. Similarly, stick to the point with your scenes; don't allow yourself to get sidetracked into another scene midway through. Address and resolve the point of tension at hand before moving on to the next one.

Hiatuses and segues

There are two methods used to move from one scene to another: hiatuses and segues. A **hiatus** indicates a passage in time or a change of character/setting, and is indicated by a double space that separates your scenes. When you finish one scene, you simply tap the return key twice, and then start the next one. Hiatuses are my personal preference, as they allow you to progress smoothly through a story with no lags, moving directly from action piece to action piece like a film. The only real drawback to hiatuses is that they can feel somewhat jumpy if your scenes are very short; if this is the case, you might want to use a segue to link shorter scenes, and use hiatuses for longer ones.

A **segue** is a bit of narrative that links your scenes, allowing you to flow smoothly from one to the other. The trick with segues is not to get too carried away with them; they're simply linking devices, and should be kept brief. For instance, you might have something like:

> *That night I slept fitfully, shivering in my bedroll on the hard ground. When I woke the next morning, I could smell sausages cooking. I peeked out of my blankets and saw Griswold the dwarf scowling over his frying pan, the smoke curling upwards into the leaves.*

However, there must then be a *definite scene* between the main character and Griswold. One danger of using segues is that unless you are certain of what you wish to accomplish with your scenes, they can tempt you down the path of sloppy writing: following along with the main character as she takes a leisurely bath in the river, has a little natter with Griswold, saddles up her pony, and so on. Don't get carried away with your segues; readers don't need to know every bit of action your characters engage in. Just as with hiatuses, they should take your story from action scene to action scene.

Setting

Your story's setting is the time and place where its events occur, and it should ideally be thought through in a similar way to your characters. A strong setting almost becomes a character in its own right, adding atmosphere and a sense of reality to your work.

Just as with characters, settings can come to you in a variety of ways. You might travel to a new place and find yourself deeply inspired by it; or maybe you've always been fascinated by ancient Greece; or perhaps you decide to set your story where you live now, or in a place from your childhood. These are all valid reasons to choose a particular setting, but the trick is to match the right setting to your story. Think carefully about your story's characters and themes. A good setting should be more than just a convenient backdrop: used well, it can enhance your story and take you more deeply into it.

A good example here is in Joanne Harris's best-selling *Chocolat*, where the tiny village of Lansquenet springs into life. Though the events in the story are magical, Lansquenet feels absolutely real, down to the detailed descriptions of its cobbled streets and the doors of its church. This feeling of complete authenticity grounds us firmly in Harris's world, and allows us to suspend disbelief when the story begins taking magical turns. A strong setting was essential here: if Lansquenet had not felt so real, we would not have been able to believe in Vianne Rocher's magical chocolates.

While all stories can benefit from a strong setting, genres such as historical novels and fantasies absolutely depend on it. As a general rule, the more a story departs from modern, ordinary life, the more time and detail should be spent describing its setting. Most readers don't need much help in knowing what a high street in Slough looks like, while they might need a great deal of help envisioning an underwater thriller about sunken treasure.

You should know your story's setting intimately, so that you can bring it to life for your readers in all five senses. If you're writing about a real place you're not familiar with, go there if you can – take photos, walk its streets. Or, if travel is impossible, read all you can about your chosen setting. Approach it as you did your characters: write descriptions about it, draw maps, find out its history and geography. Even if your story is set in your hometown in the present day, don't assume that you know all there is to know about it. Spend a day or two and view it as a newcomer would, taking photos and seeing it through fresh eyes.

Research

For almost any story you write, you'll find that some amount of research is needed. In genres such as historical fiction, it will be necessary to immerse yourself in quite extensive research, while for real-life genres you might need to invest only a few days. Whatever your area of fiction, research is a valuable tool that will help readers to experience your world as real.

Research can take many forms: personal experience, talking to experts, searching the Internet, books and libraries. Though personal experience isn't always possible, it's without a doubt the best research one can do, as nothing can beat first-hand knowledge of what something feels like. Katherine Langrish, author of the popular *Troll Fell* children's series, researched her third book, *Troll Blood,* by sailing on an historically authentic Viking ship. She could have read about Viking ships for years without acquiring the vivid personal knowledge that actually sailing on one gave her (not to mention that it was probably much more fun). Similarly, books written by people who have actually worked in the fields they're writing about, as with Tom Clancy's legal thrillers, have a wonderful sense of reality to them. Their authors have been there; they know all the little details that aren't easily filled in without first-hand experience.

However, that's not to say that you shouldn't consider writing a book about scuba diving unless you hold a certificate. Talking to experts can be enlightening, and is the next best thing to experiencing something yourself. Don't be shy about seeking out experts and enquiring whether you can ask them questions – most people are delighted to share their knowledge. You should have a list of specific questions prepared, but also remember to ask a few open-ended ones, such as, 'What's the scariest thing that ever happened to you when you were scuba diving?' and 'Is there anything I haven't asked that you think I should know?' Fascinating snippets of information can occur if you just let people talk. Record the meeting if possible, or take notes, so that you won't forget important details later.

The Internet is another brilliant resource for writers – a wealth of information available with just a few clicks of your keyboard. However, be aware that the online world doesn't necessarily require someone to have credentials before they post information, so it's wise to take some of the information you find with a pinch of salt. Try to verify details across several sites, and to seek out sites written by accredited professional bodies or people who are experts in their fields. Last but not least, find books on the subject you're researching, or use your local library to get in copies of old newspapers and journals on microfiche.

Research can be a deeply intriguing pastime in its own right, so try not to get too carried away with it. Even for historical novels, a few months at the most should normally be enough to write about your chosen subject with confidence.

Remember that the truth of your story is the most important thing. If it comes down to a question of what might actually happen in real life versus a crucial plot-point that requires something else, then your story should win. You're not writing a how-to manual. Research is important to give your stories a feeling of truth, but good fiction encompasses a larger truth – and your research will sometimes need to take a backseat to that.

One important thing is that a writer must NEVER lecture his/her readers. You may find research fun and get a lot of information, but this is the tip of the iceberg thing … the reader must never get bonked about the head with your knowledge, no matter how you long to pass it on. A reader can and will skip the 'boring' bits, but the editor who decides whether or not you are going to be published reads every word, and because of the volume of work, will chuck onto the reject pile anything which is not immediately gripping. If you read your work back and find a good deal of unnecessary information, then be ruthless; cut it out, no matter how much you love it.

Katie Flynn

04

planning your story

In this chapter you will learn:
- about the value of a plan
- different techniques for planning
- that sometimes plans change.

Getting an idea for a story can be an exhilarating moment, like a diamond dropping into your hands from the sky. The creative rush and sense of excitement is like no other. When you get a story idea you're simply on top of the world, bubbling and fizzing with your wonderful secret. However, resist the urge to plunge in and begin writing immediately! An idea isn't the same thing as a story; it needs to be developed into something that works.

When it comes to this early stage of developing an idea, your notebook is invaluable. I usually write pages of notes about who my characters are and what I think might happen in their story, using the characterization exercises described in Chapter 02 as well as just scribbling down random thoughts about them and their situation. Some of the ideas that come may be ones that I use, some may not: the important thing is to not discount anything at this stage. You're gathering the story to you, piece by piece; considering all possibilities.

Try this

Children's author Jenny Alexander (*How to be a Brilliant Writer*) often uses collages when developing a story idea. Get a pile of old magazines, and keeping your story idea loosely in mind (don't think too hard about this; you want a dreamy meditative state rather than a grimly determined one), give yourself ten minutes, and tear as many images from the magazines that feel as though they have something to do with your story as you can. Some of the images may not make sense to you at first, and that's OK – trust your intuition. When you've finished, arrange the images on a piece of poster-board. Experiment with different positions, but again, don't take too long – go with your instincts. When their placement feels right to you, glue them into place. Ask yourself what the images are about as you're doing this, or talk it through with a writing friend. I've done this exercise several times, and it never fails to take me more deeply into a story, often supplying a missing puzzle piece that I've been searching for.

To plan or not to plan?

The extent to which you plan your story out before you write it is a personal choice. Some authors write their first draft with very little planning, letting the story unfold as it will. This can work if you have a solid instinctive sense of story structure, but most writers find at least some planning useful. Having read many unpublished manuscripts in my time, I can usually tell immediately those that weren't thought out beforehand, as they often have a damaging feeling of looseness and uncertainty.

> I think the biggest thing was figuring out a method that worked for me. When I started writing, I tried to write the book without all that much planning. I learned that what works for me is to develop quite a thorough plot outline before I can start writing the actual words. Showing my work to others helped me work this out.
>
> Liz Kessler

Planning aids greatly in ensuring your work has a strong inner structure, and helps you avoid writing drafts that ultimately don't work. There's nothing more discouraging than spending a year writing something, only to realize once you've finished that your novel is severely flawed and will have to be rewritten from scratch. While time spent writing is never wasted – you're always learning about your craft, and sowing creative seeds for your future works – it can be difficult to face the fact that a particular draft is hopeless.

> I plan my books very carefully, writing a detailed chapter breakdown and emotional story arc for the characters, although once I start writing I don't always stick to the breakdown of scenes rigidly; I let the interaction between the characters inform the way the story is told, although the main story arc nearly always stays the same. I like everything in a book to have relevance and so am very strict on cutting out anything that feels like padding.
>
> Linda Chapman

How much should you plan?

Though it's probably obvious that I'm an advocate of planning one's work beforehand, you do need to be careful not to plan too much. Just as a holiday can lose its enjoyment if you meticulously map out every moment of your time, a story can lose its magic if you over-plan it. Work out your main plot elements, but leave yourself room to be surprised and delighted by your characters' actions. For instance, if you know that your main character breaks into her old office at one point, you might want to leave open exactly how she does it until you reach this place in the story. Let her surprise you; you'll enjoy the writing much more this way.

Another danger of over-planning your work is that, just like talking about your novel to all and sundry, you might find that the urge to write it has inexplicably left you. When I first started planning my novels, I was so enamoured by this new tool that I went a bit hog-wild with it: I'd write single-spaced synopses 20 pages long, detailing the story scene by scene – complete with snippets of description, dialogue, characters' feelings. I wasn't writing a synopsis so much as a mini-novel, and at the end of it, the novel itself never got written, as I had no further need to write it.

Plan your story to the minimum that works for you, and save your passion for your novel. Ideally, you should know the main things that happen: the inciting event, the key plot points in Act 2, and your climax. Anything more than that, and you run the risk of losing some of the magic that makes writing such glorious fun.

Different ways of planning

Planning can take many shapes and forms, and just like characterization, there's no single right way. Experiment with the different ideas presented in this chapter, and find what works best for you. You may find that different techniques help you at different times, or that a combination of techniques works best.

Synopsis

A **synopsis** is a written summary of a story's events. There are two types of synopsis: the first is the short, formal synopsis that you send to agents and publishers in your submissions package. This is commonly written *after* you complete your story, and has nothing to do with the initial planning of it; its purpose is to let agents and publishers see the spine of your story in a few paragraphs. (How to write these synopses is covered in Chapter 11.)

The second type of synopsis is for the author's use during the planning stage, and this can be anything you want it to be. Some authors use bullet points to map out their key events; others write them almost as short stories, detailing each important scene. You can also write them using the three-act structure as a guide, breaking it down into 'set-up', 'inciting event', 'Act 2 plot points', and so on. Whatever feels most natural to you is fine, so long as your synopsis allows you to read through your story's events quickly and smoothly, getting a feel for the underlying story arc.

I tend to use synopses for the bulk of my planning. I find typing my thoughts onto a computer screen a great way to work out a story's plot points and get a sense of whether the story's tension is rising, whether cause and effect is in place, and so on. I might spend days fiddling with a synopsis, getting ideas for scenes and experimenting with putting them in different places. The three-act structure is very much at the forefront of my mind as I do this: I'm trying to craft the story's events into the shape that will feel the most dramatically satisfying.

Once I've written a synopsis that feels right to me, I'll print it up and keep it on my desk as I work, so that I can refer to it or change it if need be. By the end of the novel my plan will have become a much used document, with scribbled amendments in the margins and scenes ticked off as I write them (which gives me a nice feeling of accomplishment as I go).

Notecards

A more tactile, hands-on way to plan your story is to get some blank notecards and write your story's main events on them, one to a card. You can then spread these out in an actual storyline on the floor, arranging and re-arranging them until you have a dramatic arc that feels right to you.

This is a wonderfully versatile method, as it allows you to experiment with major changes to your story without typing a word. It's the work of a second to try a scene in a new place and see if it 'flows' better there. Similarly, it's easy to discard a scene that you suddenly realize isn't needed, or merge two scenes together, or add in a new one. You can also colour-code the cards for different plotlines, which can be helpful if you have a complex story with lots to keep track of: you can tell at a glance if a particular plotline is underdeveloped or if too much time has been spent on it.

Another advantage of notecards is that they're so portable – just put a rubber band around them, pop them in your handbag or briefcase, and you can work on your storyline whenever you like. And, it's easy for someone else to help you with it. It can often be a bit confusing and long-winded to try to tell your story to someone else for their input, but with notecards a friend can easily grasp the important elements of your story in only a few moments, and can then help you decide where your scenes are best placed, or whether some of them are even needed at all.

Personally, I tend to use notecards if I'm having a problem with my synopsis or first draft, as it's a great way to see where a story works and where its weaker elements lie. However, I know authors who swear by using notecards to plan their story in the first instance. Give it a try; see if it works for you. It's a fun, fluid way of putting a story together.

Post-it® Notes

Similar to notecards, I know authors who use Post-it® Notes to plan their story, and literally put the story's events up on the wall over their desk. They can then arrange these to form the best story arc, discarding some ideas, adding in others, using different colours if they want, and so on. The main advantage to this method is that it's so completely visual: your story is right there on the wall in front of you, laid out scene by scene. On the con side, Post-it® Notes are notorious for losing their stickiness and drifting away with an unexpected breeze! Also, you can't carry used Post-it® Notes about with you as easily as notecards.

However, just like the notecard method, using Post-it® Notes would make it easy to work through your storyline with a friend. And, they have the advantage of being somewhat whimsical, so that you're more likely to approach your story in a playful, creative mood – always a good thing!

Three-act graph

The **three-act graph**, shown opposite, is a way of graphing out your plot points to see how well they fit within the three-act structure (page 34). This can be an extremely useful tool once you've planned your storyline, as it gives you an immediate sense of your story's overall structure and where its problem areas might lie.

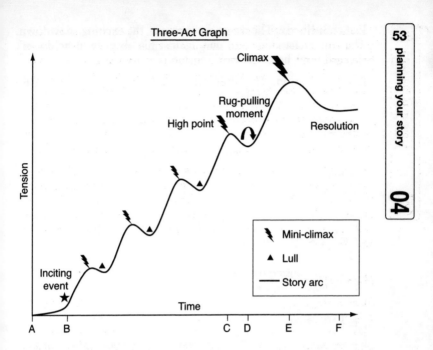

Three-Act Graph

A–F: The overall goal or problem. The entire arc covers what the main character wants, or is trying to achieve.

A–B: Act 1: the set-up. The character's ordinary life is established here, along with setting, time and place.

B: The inciting event. The event that changes everything, propelling the main character into Act 2.

B–D: Act 2: conflict. Tension is escalating as the main character strives to reach his goal or solve the problem. There are mini-climaxes and lulls as events move forward through the main character's efforts or reactions. The number of events will vary depending upon length and genre, but you should have **at least three** important plot points/attempts to overcome the problem, including C, the high point.

C: The high point. Things are looking good for the main character. He's going to succeed!

C–D: Rug-pulling moment. By a twist we never saw coming, it all goes horribly wrong.

D: The hero's darkest moment. How will he ever succeed now? End of Act 2.

E: Act 3: climax. The do-or-die moment, the exciting showdown. The hero's last chance to win against his obstacle: if he doesn't succeed now, he never will. Tension is at its highest.

E–F: Resolution. The aftermath. We briefly take stock, tie up any loose ends, and depart.

Try this

Once you've planned your story, put it on the three-act graph:

A–F: Goal or problem

A–B: Act 1: set-up

B: Inciting event

B–D: Act 2 (list important plot-points and check for cause and effect and escalating tension)

C: High point

C–D: Rug-pulling moment

D: Darkest moment

E: Act 3: climax

E–F: Resolution

How easily does it fit? If you find one particular section of the graph difficult to pinpoint or chart out, this might well be a problem area in your story. Act 2 is a common weak area (often new writers will have a lot of things happening in Act 2, but no cause and effect linking them), as is the lack of a definite goal or problem. Go back to your planning method and see if you can fix the problem. Or, now might be an ideal time to try a different planning method.

You can also use the three-act graph to map out your main character's emotional journey. Emotionally, where does your main character begin? How is he affected, step by step, by the events of Act 2, leading up to the climax? How has he changed by the end?

It's not written in stone

Being in the trenches of writing a story is very different from sitting up in HQ planning it. Once you actually start to write, you might realize that a particular scene isn't needed, or change your mind about the placement of a story event, or find that a character refuses to act in the way you thought she would. This is all fine – stay flexible and trust your instincts. Planning your story shouldn't mean that you've set it in stone. A plan is simply a guide, not a pristine document that should never be altered.

However, if you find yourself changing significant amounts, or rethinking plot points that affect the book's structural whole, then it's probably worth returning to your synopsis or getting the notecards out for an evening or two, just to make sure that your story still feels tight and strong.

It's still about character

Finally, don't ignore your characters in the midst of all this focus on story structure. Remember that it's still **their** concerns, personality traits and goals that should be driving your story forward. Planning is a means to order their story, not a device to control it: your characters always need to be in charge. Stay true to them, and you can't go far wrong.

> I think, in a way, you should find writing difficult – each new book should present a fresh challenge. I'd be very worried if I found it easy.
>
> Linda Newbery

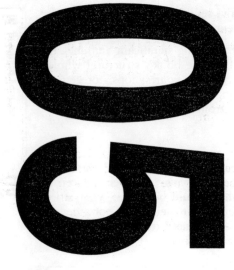

05

great openings

In this chapter you will learn:
- different techniques for story openings
- how to decide which opening is right for you.

Philip Pullman was once asked how he wrote such wonderful books. He replied that it was easy; all you have to do is write a brilliant first page. And then a brilliant second page. And then a brilliant third page, and so on until you're done. Although his answer was obviously a bit tongue in cheek, he was also completely correct. Writing riveting fiction is a matter of making every page, every *word,* as good as you can make it. No element of your story is more important than another; it all needs to be excellent.

However, your opening does have more pressure placed on it than the rest of your story, because it's the first thing agents and readers will look at. And if they don't like it, they're unlikely to read on. Your opening should act as an irresistible invitation that draws readers into your world and makes them want to keep reading. There are several different ways you can accomplish this, or you can use a mix of these techniques:

- presenting an out-of-the-ordinary situation
- posing an essential question
- plunging into an exciting action sequence
- interesting use of language
- using a strong, appealing voice.

An out-of-the-ordinary situation

A book that opened from the point of view of a foetus in the womb might well grab a reader's attention, simply because it's so unusual. Similarly, a book that opened with the main character hang-gliding off a cliff might keep a reader turning pages, too.

A good example of a striking opening is William Golding's classic novel *Lord of the Flies.* Golding begins his novel with a fair-haired boy scrambling over the rocks beside a lagoon; we quickly find out that he and another boy who appear are English schoolboys, stranded without adults on a tropical island. We are immediately intrigued by their situation, and want to find out more. Many authors might have been tempted to begin the story prior to the crash, but Golding's choice draws us much more immediately into the isolation and strangeness of his world. (Note that this is an example of a novel which starts *after* the inciting event – the plane crash that left the boys on the island – and that the tension continues to build from there up to the shattering climax.)

However, you must play fair with your readers. If you open with your main character as a matador in a bullring, this had better be an intrinsic part of your story. You should never draw a reader in this way only to then have something like, '"Well, that was fun," Tom said to Margaret as he tossed the red cape to an attendant. "What a great holiday this is turning out to be! What shall we do next?"'

Your readers could be excused at this point for shoving your book back onto the shelf in disgust. Any opening you use needs to grow organically from your characters and your storyline, but if you can find a way to start things off in a fresh, unusual way, then by all means use it.

Posing an essential question

This doesn't mean that you literally open your story by asking a question; rather, that your action begins in such a way that the reader instantly demands to know what happens next. An example of this is in David Gemmell's best-selling fantasy novel *Waylander,* which opens with this line: 'They had begun to torture the priest when the stranger stepped from the shadows of the trees.'

Whether you like fantasy or not, I think most people would find it almost impossible to put the book down at that point. There are too many vital questions that we immediately want answered: Who are 'they'? Why were they torturing a priest? Who is the stranger? And, most importantly, *what happened next?*

Another example is in *Wolf Brother* by Michele Paver. Paver opens her blockbuster children's novel with her main character, Torak, huddled in the undergrowth, terrified that the bear that severely wounded his father will come back. Immediately, we're worried on Torak's behalf, wondering: *Will* the bear come back? Will Torak's father live? What's going to happen?

The goal of a blockbuster opening is to make it so compelling that it's impossible for a reader to put your book down. Grabbing their attention with a strong situation that immediately raises questions is a great way to do this.

Exciting action sequence

Propelling your reader straight into the action is another common blockbuster opening, such as in James Patterson's best-selling thriller *When the Wind Blows*. Patterson begins his novel with Max, an eleven-year-old girl, escaping from the strange school or prison that's been holding her and her brother captive. We don't know why at this point – a master of suspense, Patterson holds back the truth about Max's identity until later in the story – but from the first moment, we're riveted as Max dodges through the trees, frantically avoiding the men with guns who pursue her. We're frightened on Max's behalf, and desperate to know what happens next. In this case, Max's escape is the inciting event that sets the rest of the story in motion.

You can also start with exciting action that has nothing to do with the inciting event. In Philippa Gregory's best-selling historical novel *The Other Boleyn Girl,* we open with the protagonist, Mary, watching the execution of her uncle, the Duke of Buckinghamshire. Incongruously, thirteen-year-old Mary is bored; she's certain that the king will grant clemency to her uncle at the last moment, and wishes he'd hurry up about it so that everyone can go home. When the Duke is instead beheaded by the executioner's axe, Mary is stunned and sickened. The scene is a gripping opening, essential in terms of Mary's character growth, and draws us vividly into the brutal world of Tudor England.

Again, though, be careful that you don't insert a red herring here; whatever action sequence you open with should be germane to your plot. And, make sure that you don't neglect character for action. By all means, open with a tense bank robbery, but give your reader something to connect with: make sure that they're in the viewpoint of one of the characters, so that they can feel vitally involved with what's going on.

Interesting use of language

Some novels draw readers in through their use of language. For instance, in Jay McInerney's best-selling *Bright Lights, Big City*, his innovative device of writing the book in the second person instantly catches the reader's notice. Another example can be found in Alice Walker's brilliant novel *The Color Purple*. Written in the form of letters, Celie, the uneducated protagonist, pours her heart out to God in her own words. Walker remains true to how Celie would phrase and spell things, and the occasional misspellings and lack of punctuation work almost lyrically here, adding greatly to the book's poignancy and power.

However, the most important thing is that your writing should feel natural and smooth, so don't attempt innovations as an attention-getting device. If you do plan to bend or explore the rules of grammar, be very sure that you know what you're doing and why you're doing it.

Sometimes the sheer beauty and power of an author's use of language can draw readers in. In Joanne Harris's *Chocolat,* the rich, vivid description of a French carnival catches the imagination and sweeps the reader into the story. By the time the action begins a few pages later, we are deliciously under the lush spell of Harris's writing. However, while this works wonderfully in *Chocolat*, it can be a mistake to rely on the beauty of your words to carry your opening. Try to have something else going on too, so that your readers are sure to keep turning pages.

Strong character voice

Particularly in first-person novels, a strong character voice can be the driving force that propels a reader into your story. An example here is J. D. Salinger's classic novel *The Catcher in the Rye*. Told in the first-person voice of Holden Caulfield, Salinger's opening propels us directly into his hero's mind, as his youthful and irreverent voice informs us that we shouldn't read this book if we want to know anything about his parents, or his background, or any of that 'David Copperfield kind of crap'. Holden's voice carries the opening, and indeed the novel.

A more contemporary example can be found in Mark Haddon's crossover best-seller *The Curious Incident of the Dog in the Night-Time*. The main character, a teenage boy called Christopher, has Asperger's Syndrome, a form of autism that means he cannot understand human emotions. Christopher views the world in terms of maths and science, and his unique first-person voice is undoubtedly what has made this novel such an immense success. Though Haddon starts with action – Christopher's discovery that the next-door poodle has been stabbed with a garden fork (which is also the story's inciting event) – it is Christopher's voice that really grabs our attention and draws us in, as we quickly realize from his detailed, careful logic that he is not viewing this disturbing event as most people would. We read on, fascinated by the workings of his mind, and touched by his efforts to make sense of the incomprehensible people around him.

Which opening is right for you?

The opening to strive for is probably a combination of some of the techniques described above. Don't depend *solely* on a great character voice or beautiful writing: add gripping action, a vital question or an unusual situation as well.

The key is also to start where your story starts. This sounds easy, but it can be tricky to know exactly where this is at times. However, if you're writing a crime thriller about a diamond heist which is told from the thief's point of view, you probably don't want to begin with the car accident she was in when she was three, or her first kiss, or her disappointment at not getting into the university of her choice. After doing the character exercises recommended, these may all be things that you know are vital parts of your character's background, and they might come out later (though they don't have to; they could remain important background that only you know about) – but they probably don't have anything to do with where your story begins.

Knowing your story's structure can help greatly. Decide on the inciting event, and start as close to it as possible, keeping differences of genre in mind. (For instance, teenage fiction may start a matter of paragraphs before the inciting event, while adult science fiction may start a chapter or two before it.) Or, you can start with your inciting event and fill in details about the set-up and back-story later on, when and if these are needed.

Though this breakdown of openings may make the process seem mechanical, the best openings are anything but, growing organically from characters and situation. The main thing to remember is that your story's opening should interest and excite, from the very first sentence if possible. You want your reader to be happily helpless, so caught up in the spell of your story that they'll eagerly keep reading to see what happens next. Stay firmly in your main character's heart and mind, think about the most interesting place your story could begin, and let your instincts take over from there.

Try this

Look at ten of your favourite books, and make a note of how the authors handled the opening. Did they use the techniques described; a combination of them? Get a feel for your favourite type of opening. What really excites you, and draws you right into a story? Character voice? An unusual situation?

Keeping this in mind, write five brilliant openings in your notebook. You don't have to know what the stories are, just write five brilliant openings. Work on honing and perfecting them, making them as gripping as possible.

06

how to write blockbuster prose

In this chapter you will learn:
- the difference between active and passive writing
- ways to keep your writing active
- the value of assessing your own work.

Blockbuster fiction is about connecting with your readers. This is done in a variety of ways – great characters, a riveting storyline, tense situations. Weaving through all of these story aspects is the concept of active writing, otherwise known as 'show, don't tell', which draws your reader directly into the action, so that they feel they're living it for themselves.

In contrast, when your characters and situations are primarily 'told', there is often a tangible barrier between your reader and the story. It's the difference between participating in an exciting event yourself and listening to a deadpan newsreader read a commentary of the event on TV. Novels that 'tell' too much can feel flat and are often frustrating to read. Personally, I've been known to throw such books across the room in my time. (At the very least, I grit my teeth.)

Show, don't tell

Show, don't tell – or SDT, as I usually scribble in the margins of manuscripts I read – is a concept best explained through example. So before we do anything else, consider this passage:

Jaz felt her foot slip, and a moment later she had fallen over the side of the cliff. She grabbed with one hand, and managed to catch hold of a tree root as she fell. Her descent was stopped. She was hanging by one hand, with a sheer drop below her. She was completely terrified. The tree root felt unstable, and if it didn't hold her weight, she would fall to her death – and no one knew where she was. She looked up. The cliff edge was at least ten feet up, with no footholds or handholds in sight. She was doomed.

What do you think of this? Take a few seconds to quickly note down your immediate thoughts – maybe just a few words that sum this piece of writing up for you. How did it make you feel when you were reading it?

Finished? OK. Let's look at Jaz's problem again:

Jaz's foot shot out from under her, and she fell over the side of the cliff. Grab something, anything! A jolt slammed through her as her flailing hand found a tree root. And then the only sound was the roaring in her ears, and the pattering of dirt and falling rocks. Jaz swallowed, her muscles shrieking as the world turned slowly below.

She could see tiny dots of sheep grazing in the distance.
The tree root creaked as she glanced up, stinging her face
with a fresh shower of dirt. The cliff edge rose in a sheer,
steep face, at least ten feet above her. And nobody knew
where she was.

Again, take a few seconds to write down your impressions.
What, for you, is the main difference between this piece of
writing and the first one? What sort of words would you use to
describe this second piece? How did it make you feel?

The first piece of writing – as I'm sure you've guessed – is an
example of passive, 'telling' writing. I'd be surprised if you
preferred it to the second piece, or thought it did a better job in
bringing the scene to life. Since the situation being described in
both pieces is tense, you were probably at least somewhat
interested as you read the first one – but did you really
feel engaged with Jaz's predicament? Did your breath catch in
your throat?

Mine certainly didn't as I was writing it. In contrast, I was
completely connected with the second piece of writing. I *was* Jaz
– in her mind and in her body as she hung there, experiencing
first-hand what she could feel, see, hear: the racing of her
heartbeat, the sour taste of panic in her mouth. I had to stretch
my writing muscles and transport myself directly into the scene,
striving to report back to you exactly what Jaz was experiencing.

And, as is vital in show, don't tell, I didn't sum anything up for
you. I didn't *tell* you that Jaz was terrified, or about to fall to
her death; I *showed* you terror and danger instead, without
making any comment about them at all. You were left to make
your own connections. This is the essence of show, don't tell. In
general, anything that propels the story forward should be
shown (ideally, most of the book). However, there are places
where telling might be more appropriate, such as segues
between scenes (covered in Chapter 03).

You'll find published books that don't use show, don't tell, and
some of them are extremely successful. These books normally
have riveting storylines and excellent characterization – in other
words, their other elements are strong enough to bolster a lack
of vivid writing. You shouldn't count on this for your own work
– it's a tough market out there, and you should strive to make
every aspect of your writing as powerful as possible.

The most common mistake for new writers seems to be 'telling not showing' – pages and pages of describing what's happening rather than getting stuck into the action are a big no-no.

Carole Matthews

The alpha state

Often when writing, I'm in a state of concentration so intense that the rest of the world just drops away. I'm not simply *imagining* the scenes I'm writing about; I've entered into them myself, and can see, hear, feel, taste and touch them. This is 'the alpha state' – a slowed-down level of consciousness somewhere between dreaming and being awake. Entering into the alpha state is essential to producing active writing. If you yourself don't feel that you're living the things you're writing about, then you won't be able to convince a reader of them.

Try this

Write a scene describing an emotional event from your childhood – but before you start to write, just sit quietly for a moment with your eyes closed, placing yourself back in that time and place. What do you see? What do you feel emotionally? What are the sounds, smells and tastes? What is your body language like? What about the body language of others?

When you feel deeply within the scene, open your eyes and begin to write. Keep your concentration on the images and sensations as you do so. Strive to show them to your readers as sharply and truthfully as you can, without summing up any conclusions about what's going on. Leave it to your readers to make their own connections.

Let's look now at some of the different ways you can use show, don't tell to bring your work to life.

Use action verbs/sentence structure

'Was' and 'were' are passive verbs, and since this chapter is all about *active* writing, you can probably infer that using passive verbs is not the key to this! A painful excess of 'was' and 'were' litter many of the manuscripts I've seen from beginner writers (and sometimes more experienced ones as well), and the cumulative effect is almost always to drag the story down and bury it in passivity.

A quick definition might be useful here:

Passive: The new author was signed on by a top publisher.
Active: A top publisher signed on the new author.

A sentence is **passive** when its subject ('author') is acted upon ('was signed on'). In an **active** sentence the subject ('publisher') is acting ('signed on'). But leaving the grammar lesson aside, do you see the emotional difference between the two examples? One pulls you right into the action, the other just tells you about it. Which feels fresher and more immediate?

In my own writing, this is something I try to be very aware of. If I find myself composing a sentence with 'was' or 'were', whenever possible I turn it around and rewrite it using an active construction instead. It's always more powerful and interesting that way; I honestly can't think of an exception. When your writing is primarily passive, the reader's eye tends to skim lightly over your story, taking in only the surface of your words, and remaining unaffected by them emotionally.

Try this

Think back to your first kiss (or imagine what it might be like, if it's yet to occur), and write several pages about exactly how it happened.

Now, read over what you've written, and underline every passive verb. How many do you have? Don't worry if it's a lot; this is easily done. Rewrite the piece, and this time strive to eliminate every passive verb. Compare the two versions. Which do you like better? Which feels as though it draws you in more, bringing the scene to life?

Have another quick scan of Jaz as she dangles from the cliff face in the two examples at the start of this chapter. Note that in the first passage, the dreaded 'was' appears over and over, keeping us cushioned firmly outside of the action. In the second example, the writing is almost entirely active instead, with only one passive verb. Make direct statements with your writing instead of soggy, indirect ones. 'Was' and 'were' are soggy, and if you have too many of them in a story it can start to feel like the author wrote it while buried under a heavy blanket. (However, you of course do have to use 'was' and 'were' sometimes, so don't go into contortions to avoid them, which can be painful to read in themselves.)

Avoid adverbs and 'emotion' words

Adverbs are words that modify the action a verb takes, and commonly end in '-ly'. You're probably most familiar with them as ways to describe how a character is feeling, or how they said a line of dialogue: 'happily', 'sarcastically', 'despondently'. They're quick, they're easy … and they're lazy writing. Don't succumb. You can do much better than this, and your readers will be drawn more deeply into your world as a result. As an example, here's a short passage from my novel *Breakfast at Sadie's*:

> *'I thought maybe I'd stay at home today.' I put the dishes onto the counter.*
>
> *Aunt Leona stood at the sink, splashing water about as she did the dishes. She glared at the new ones I had just brought in. 'Oh, ta for that.'*

Look at Aunt Leona's body language: her glare; the way she's splashing the water about. How sincere do you think her thanks are? Yet I don't have to *say* 'she said sarcastically', and it would feel over-obvious and unneeded if I did. Too many adverbs 'dumb down' your writing. They're a crutch used when you're unsure of your writing powers, and are afraid that your characters aren't getting your meanings across on their own. However, if you've considered your characters in as much detail as recommended in Chapter 02, then they're more than capable of doing the job themselves.

> *'What do you mean by that?' he said belligerently.*
>
> *'What the bloody hell do you mean by that?' His hands coiled into fists.*

In the first sentence, the word 'belligerent' is the only clue we have that the line of dialogue was said in an aggressive manner. In context, it's weak dialogue, because it couldn't stand on its own without explanation. However, in the second example, the dialogue instantly springs into focus as being belligerent, particularly with the addition of hostile action. We no longer need to be *told* 'belligerent', we have been shown it much more effectively through the character's dialogue and movements.

Similarly, and for the same reasons, try to avoid using the word for an emotion to get across how your characters are feeling. Instead of saying 'He was elated,' find a way to show this to your readers through your character's dialogue, actions and physical sensations. How does elation feel? What does it look like? Imagine that you're watching a film. You don't need subtitles appearing that let us know how the characters feel; if someone's elated, we know it from their tone, from their expression, from body language, from what we know of the character. This is what you should be striving for in your writing, as well.

Try this

Write a short story about the worst day in someone's life. Without using a single adverb or word for an emotion, make it clear to your reader exactly what the character is going through. (By the way, it's cheating to have the character say, 'This is truly the worst day of my life'!)

Like passive verbs, too many adverbs and emotion words keep readers on the surface of your story. They are a quick spoon-feeding of what's going on, requiring no mental effort from your reader. And although film and books are different media, we should be striving to give our readers the same freedom to infer things on their own, to give them that split-second thrill in the air that a trapeze artist experiences before they grasp the bar. Put the needed clues in place, nudge your readers in the right direction with pertinent actions and strong dialogue – and keep your authorial conclusions and summing-ups ('happily', 'sarcastically', 'sad') out of it.

I have a real fear of boring people and so tend to pare everything down as far as possible. I also hate adverbs, and am starting to dislike adjectives almost as much! Small gestures in a character can be so revealing.

Meg Rosoff

Choosing the perfect word

Strive to find the *one perfect word* that means precisely what you want to express, as this sort of attention to detail can greatly help to bring your images to life. Think about what you're trying to say, and what word would perfectly describe it.

If you can use a word that's slightly unusual in context, so much the better. You don't want to use words that are so bizarre that they jolt your reader out of your story, but you do want to keep things fresh and exciting for them. One of my favourite examples of this is from a book called *Red Azalea,* by Anchee Min. The main character is jogging with some soldiers in a gruelling survival course, and she says 'their footsteps chopped through me'. I love that, because you can both hear and feel the effect of their pounding footsteps on the ground.

But even with more everyday language, using the word that means exactly what you're trying to say can liven things up considerably:

He walked quietly across the room, taking care that he wasn't heard.

He crept across the room.

In the first sentence, a lot of explanation has to take place to modify the verb 'walked', since you can 'walk' pretty much any way under the sun. As a result, the sentence feels wordy, striving too hard for effect. However, when you substitute the word that actually *means* 'walking quietly, trying not to be heard', the image springs into focus. The writing instantly feels tighter and less laboured, and it's also able to take a backseat to what's actually going on. We're not forced to wait until the sentence is over to figure out how the character is moving; *boom,* we know instantly, and we can keep flowing with the story, wrapped snugly within it. The more you can hone your writing so that it's an innocuous background voice, there only to aid your characters and guide the action, the more your story will leap into life.

The bottom line is to try to make the writing as transparent as possible, to make yourself as author disappear from the mind of the reader. Load as much of yourself as you want into the characters, but make sure the audience is spending time with them, not you.

Michael Marshall Smith

Here's another example, this time in sentences of similar length:

> *Sue's feet skated out from under her, and she crashed onto the ice.*

> *Sue slipped on the ice and lost her footing, falling backwards onto the ground.*

Was there a small 'ouch' when you read one of the sentences? If so, I bet it wasn't the second one, where the writing feels conservative and stilted. The word choices are commonplace, and the action is almost painfully described, step by step (or slip by slip). Reading it doesn't feel at all like falling on the ice, because there's no jolting moment of impact – everything is very carefully laid out for us, so that by the time Sue actually hits the ground, we're not even surprised.

In the first sentence, there's more freedom – the image has been opened up, allowing readers to experience it for themselves. Note the slight leap of trust involved: the author trusts that the reader will fill in that gap between slipping and falling, without their having to painstakingly state 'and lost her footing'.

Looking at the language, it's more interesting and direct. 'Slipping' and 'falling' *can* be perfect words in other contexts, but are they the right ones here? 'She slipped and fell on the ice' sounds somewhat meek and timid, as though the author is apologizing for even putting such an idea forward. Be bold! She 'skated'. She 'crashed'. These words are much more evocative of what falling on the ice actually feels like, and therefore allow readers to enter more easily into the scene, and wince along with the hapless Sue.

A corollary to using the perfect word is to use sharp, specific detail:

> *Jo took a sip of delicious white wine.*

> *Jo took a sip of cool, crisp Chardonnay.*

Words like delicious, beautiful, etc. are meaningless as description, because they're so subjective. My idea of delicious or beautiful may not be yours. So although we're told the wine is delicious in the first sentence, this is vague, fuzzy writing that will do little to tantalize your readers' taste buds. Specific details bring your writing to life, like adjusting a camera lens so that your readers can see clearly what's going on.

Consider every word you write with great care. Is it the most evocative? Does it mean exactly what you meant to say? Sometimes the first word that comes to mind is the perfect one, but often it's just the one that's easy and convenient. Try to push yourself, and think of phrasings that are more original and arresting.

Try this

Choose an object, and write down the ten most obvious words that you might use to describe it. For instance, a rose might be 'red', 'thorned', 'sweet-smelling' and so on. Now, write a paragraph describing your object without using any of the ten words. Push yourself to find new ways of viewing it, with fresh word choices to mirror these.

Exposition through dialogue/incident

I've seen many manuscripts where the author zipped over the surface of what was happening in a sort of glib running commentary rather than entering into the scene and showing readers what was happening for themselves. If your novel is full of passages like the following, it might well be too skimpy, and need fleshing out:

> *Once again, Keith was playing his music at full blast, driving his mother to distraction. She pounded on the ceiling and asked him to quit, but he turned it up louder. So she went up to his room and demanded that he turn it down.*

Now the fleshed-out version:

> *BOOM! BOOM! BOOM-TIKKA-BOOM!*
>
> *'Not again!' moaned Anna. Grabbing a broomstick, she pounded the ceiling, sending flakes of plaster drifting down. 'Keith! Turn off the bloody noise!'*
>
> *BOOM BOOM BOOM!*
>
> *'I know you can hear me!' Anna sprinted up the stairs. The wall of sound was like fighting her way through a snowstorm. She rattled his doorknob. Locked. Again. (She didn't even want to know what he was doing in there.)*

'Keith!'

No answer.

Pound, pound, pound on his door. 'KEITH, ANSWER ME!'

All at once the sound stopped, like a gushing tap being turned off. The door opened a crack, and a single blue eye peered out.

'What?'

Anna took a deep breath. 'Keith. My darling son, love of my life. Turn off your music or I'm going to kill you.'

Which does a better job of bringing the scene to life? Just as importantly, which is simply more fun to read? Note that I didn't have to use any words like 'angry' or 'frustrated'. Anna's actions and dialogue got these ideas across in a far more effective and interesting way. In general, if something is important enough to *tell* your readers about, you should consider letting your characters *show* the action instead. Snap your readers right into the scene, and let them see it for themselves.

I try to take the advice handed out by the editor of the *London Evening Standard*, who told me that 'flashbacks are the death of commuter interest', e.g. a chap standing in the tube or in a train can only cope with straightforward narrative. So as far as possible I cut out the 'She thought back over her recent encounter with him,' and make it happen before their very eyes.

Katie Flynn

Get inside your main character's head

You want your readers to identify and sympathize with your main character, and regardless of whether you're writing in the first or third person, this necessitates getting inside your hero's head. Show us his world from his eyes, and in his voice.

However, if you're writing in the first person, don't assume that this automatically means you're writing in an active, showing way. First-person voice can very easily slide into telling instead, i.e.

I was so angry! I couldn't believe that my own sister would do that to me. How could she? She knew how hurt I had been ever since Mum's death…'

This is all 'telling', because the character isn't thinking so much as summing up what's going on for the reader. The same rules that we've been talking about still apply in the first person voice: give your readers the clues they need to make the connections themselves, and no more. (And don't tell them 'angry and hurt', show it to them instead!) For instance:

> *I stared at her, shaking. The bitch! How could she have done this to me? Especially after Mum ... I cleared my throat, holding back the tears. 'Right. Well, I'm sorry you feel that way.'*

Internal voice means that your readers should feel and hear what a character would actually be feeling and thinking at any particular moment; it shouldn't be used as a handy way to sum things up and spoon-feed them to the reader. To do this effectively, you need to be firmly inside your main character's mind. It's just as important to do this when using the third person, both through echoing your character's thoughts in your narration and by letting your reader hear her internal voice.

> *God, what a day. Nancy put on Schubert's 'Death and the Maiden' – yeah, and that's how I feel, too, she thought, collapsing on her bed. Hardly a maiden any more, though. She smiled.*

Though we're in third person, the reader can still hear Nancy's thoughts, gaining a flash of humour and insight into how the character thinks.

Don't let third-person writing act as a barrier between your main character and your readers. While one of the advantages of third person is that the narrative camera can pull back and show readers your hero from the outside (as discussed in Chapter 02), they shouldn't feel trapped out there. The trick is to flavour your narrative with how your main character herself would state things. Let her voice shine through and take the lead, and don't be afraid to dip into her thoughts.

Use of metaphors/similes

A simile is a comparison using 'like' or 'as', such as: 'The crouching cat was like a panther.' A metaphor is a comparison that says something is something else, such as: 'The night sky was black velvet studded with diamonds.' Don't go overboard and start using metaphors and similes in every other sentence, as too many of them will clutter up your work rather than enhance it – the reader begins to notice your writing instead of the story. However, used sparingly, metaphors and similes can be an excellent way to spice up your writing and show your reader something rather than telling it:

> *Polly's stomach was a ball of writhing snakes.*

> *The man's voice was like crumbling chalk.*

> *Her feet were delicate white seashells, curving gently into her shoes.*

In a manuscript I once read, the author described an old man on walking sticks looking 'about as mobile as a clamped car'. I thought this was a brilliant use of simile – a fresh, punchy image that perfectly described the character's difficulty in moving, and hinted also at the frustrations involved. Young children often use wonderful similes and metaphors. A ten-year old I once taught described a tiger's coat as being covered in 'black lightning'. Perfect.

Be careful not to slip into clichés, though. Often when a phrase pops easily into your mind, it's good to be suspicious of it: 'jet-black hair', 'a babbling brook', 'a roaring fire'. These were fresh and new once, but have long since lost any ability to transport readers into a scene. Strive to use language in an original way; clichés that people have heard a hundred times before will do nothing to make an image really come to life in their minds.

The best writing puts a unique spin on things, and shows the reader an image in a new, unexpected way that feels perfectly right. Using language in such a fresh way often means viewing the world around you as though you have never seen it before. Notice the little details, and strive to find bright, original ways to describe them.

Try this

The next time you go shopping, notice the wonderful array of fruits and vegetables on display – their different colours, shapes, smells and textures. Really study them, as though you've never seen them before: the rich purple of an aubergine; the dimpled flesh of an orange. Choose ten of your favourites, and write similes or metaphors for each one. The aubergine might be like a wealthy woman's purse, or the orange a teardrop from the sun. Strive to describe each fruit or vegetable in a fresh new way that feels exactly right.

Showing *and* telling

Writers new to show, don't tell often go through an interim stage where they're both showing *and* telling their work. They're learning how to show their story's action, but they don't quite trust the process yet, and so they can't resist tacking on explanations as well. The result might look something like this:

> *Juan slowly creaked open the door. His heart turned to ice as he took in the scene before him – scattered bodies, blood, the utter carnage left behind by a madman. He was terrified. Clutching his gun, he moved forward, edging into the room. The cold metal felt slick in his hands.*
>
> *Suddenly he heard a noise, and he whirled around, his pulse slamming against his temples. 'Hands up!' he barked.*

This feels as though the writer is on the right track, but needs to push himself just that bit more. A good rewrite of this passage, employing everything we've discussed, might look like this:

> *Juan* ~~*slowly*~~ *creaked open the door,* and *his heart turned to ice.* ~~*as he took in the scene before him*~~*.* Three bodies lay sprawled in the room in dark pools of blood – two women and a man, all of them wearing business clothes. Their throats gaped open like extra mouths. ~~*scattered bodies, blood the utter carnage left behind by a madman. He was terrified.*~~ *Clutching his gun,* Juan ~~*moved forward, edging*~~ edged *into the room,* trying not to gag. *The cold metal felt slick in his hands.*
>
> ~~*Suddenly he heard a noise, and he*~~ A scraping noise came from behind him. He *whirled around,* ~~*his*~~ pulse slamming against his temples. 'Hands up!' he barked.*

Here's a quick breakdown of what I've done:

- 'slowly': we don't need this as 'creaking' open the door implies that it was done slowly. Plus it's one of those wretched adverbs, so we scorn it on general principle.
- 'as he took in the scene before him': the reader can infer this on their own from the context – in one sentence he's opening the door, in the next there are bodies lying in the room. Juan is obviously looking at them, so spelling this out isn't needed.

- 'scattered bodies, blood': most of the rewriting had to do with adding specific detail – there was very little in the first version. We're told only that there are scattered bodies and blood. By entering more deeply into the scene and describing the bodies, they become human, and more disturbing and powerful.
- 'the utter carnage left behind by a madman': this has no place here, as it's the author butting in to give a judgment on what's happened – in effect, waving a placard in the air and telling the reader what to think. 'Warning, warning! Madman on the loose!' Not needed. If you describe the scene well enough, your readers will think exactly what you want them to, without your having to spell it out for them, and it will have a much stronger impact as a result.
- 'He was terrified': this sentence is redundant in context. We can figure this out more powerfully from Juan's body language – his heart turning to ice, etc.
- 'moved forward, edging into the room': redundant, so I chose the stronger image. I added 'trying not to gag' because I felt that we could have just a touch more insight into how Juan was physically feeling as he viewed the scene.
- 'suddenly he heard a noise': 'suddenly' is one of those words – sometimes it works, and sometimes it serves only to cushion the surprise for the reader. It felt better without it here. And, instead of just 'a noise', I added a bit more detail, describing what the noise sounded like.

Practice makes perfect

Once you've been introduced to show, don't tell as a concept, the realization that you're telling instead of showing your work usually happens in stages. Perhaps you'll be looking over a paragraph when you'll suddenly see something like 'She was really angry', and wonder how you could have possibly missed this before. So you'll go back and work on the scene some more, working on showing us angry instead, and then in the next draft you might notice a few other 'tolds' lurking in the same passage: 'she said shortly', 'he replied with a sneer in his tone'. The process of discovering and replacing the 'telling' in your work is very like peeling an onion. The more you find, the deeper into the scene you can go.

Action plan for active writing

Once you've begun writing a novel, go through one of your chapters and notice every instance where you've used a passive verb (was/were) construction. Rewrite these in an active way instead. Often this means completely rethinking the sentence: 'He was furious, and knew he'd never speak to her again' obviously needs a bit more work than simply re-jigging it without the verb 'was'. If you start to get a feel for how glib and emotionally limiting an overuse of 'was' and 'were' is – and how rewriting in an active form plunges you more deeply into your scenes, and makes you think more – then you're on the right track.

Next, notice every time that you've used the word for how a character is feeling. (If you've never encountered this concept before, there will probably be a lot of these!) Get rid of as many as you can, and instead, strive to *show* us how your character is feeling, without actually saying the word. Again, you should start to get a sense for how much more deeply you, the author, must enter into your scenes and your characters' heads when writing this way. As you do this, you should also start noticing your use of language, and begin pushing yourself to ensure that every word is the perfect one.

Finally, look out for instances where you've told the reader what's going on in the story itself. These can be hard to spot at first, but will probably look something like, 'This was truly the happiest day of Frank's life. It could never get better than this.' Or, 'Jake and Samantha crouched on the ridge, staring down at the enemy camp. They exchanged a glance that said what they both knew: they were in terrible danger. One false move, and they'd be dead.'

If your readers can't figure out on their own that this is the happiest day of Frank's life, or don't have a clue that Jake and Sam are in terrible danger up on that ridge, then your story is in dire straits, and isn't going to be saved by supplying them with this information on a plate. Remember that readers have to *feel it for themselves for it to be effective*. This can be scary for an author at first, because it means giving up control – what if you leave the reader to figure things out on their own, and they don't get it? Don't worry. If you've done your job right, they will, and your writing will gain the sort of resonance that makes a story linger in the mind long after it has been put down.

Finally...

Probably everything that you've read in this chapter makes perfect sense to you – but be warned, it's perfectly possible to write a passage while thinking *show, show, show,* and then read it over later to find that it's all told instead. Don't panic. It just takes time and practice. And the more you practise it, the more richly enjoyable your writing will become – because at its heart, show, don't tell means that you're going deeply within yourself to enter into your stories. You're living and breathing them, and then coming back and relaying their truth to us, unadorned and free of judgment, so that we can live and breathe them on our own.

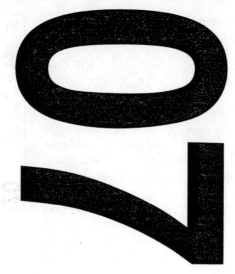

07
dialogue

In this chapter you will learn:
- how to get your characters talking
- how to avoid the pitfalls of dialogue-writing
- how to make dialogue count.

It's tempting to make this a very short chapter, and say that if you follow the advice in Chapter 02 about getting to know your characters, then all you have to do to write great dialogue is sit back and let them talk to each other – their speech will flow naturally on its own. However, while getting to know your characters helps tremendously in writing natural dialogue, it's not quite the whole story. Some general guidelines are helpful.

What makes good dialogue?

First, good dialogue does *not* strive to sound precisely like how people talk in real life. If you've ever listened in on someone talking on their mobile, or read through a court transcript, then you'll know what a painful experience real-life dialogue can be at times – littered with 'hems' and 'haws' and 'ums' and 'you knows' and pointless repetition. Dialogue that mimicked this exactly would be tedious to read.

Nor does good dialogue have to be 'proper' speech. Gramatically speaking, though most of us know how things should be said, few of us employ these rules in our everyday conversations. So if you have your characters saying things to each other like, 'Oh, hello, Murgatroyd. I did not know you were going to be here today. Do you plan to stay very long?' then readers can infer that the speaker is either embalmed (and stiffening alarmingly further by the second), or that he learned English from a foreign phrases book, and no one's had the heart to set him straight yet.

On the whole, real people just don't talk this way. They use contractions and incomplete sentences; they interrupt themselves. Something like, 'Murgatroyd! Blimey, I didn't know you were coming today – how long are you staying?' would sound much more true to life. Good dialogue is a compromise. While it should be 'proper' enough to be read easily, it should also be relaxed and natural-sounding.

If you think your dialogue sounds stiff, using your notebook on a regular basis is an excellent way to improve your skills. Write down snippets of interesting conversation; vivid turns of phrase; note how different people put their words together. You'll start to get a feel for how people talk to each other, and how you can use this to loosen up your characters' speech.

Try this

The next time you're in a public place, unobtrusively eavesdrop on someone's conversation (and if you're caught, I did not tell you to do this). In your writer's notebook, write down some of the overheard dialogue as exactly as you can, 'ums' and 'uhs' and all. Read through it: would this be good story dialogue? Work at polishing and streamlining it, keeping a loose, relaxed feel but getting rid of any irritating redundancies or hesitations. Keep reworking it until it feels natural and easy to read.

When you're finished, read it out loud. Does it flow as naturally as you thought? Tailor it a bit more if not. Reading your dialogue out loud is an excellent way to pick up on any awkward word choices or general stiffness.

I could always 'do' descriptive writing, even as a child – and I've been writing since I was a child. I found dialogue the next hurdle – and I think I overcame that by keeping a notebook and jotting down conversations. I did that for years, off and on – and it does help. You have to find out how to prune the untidiness of everyday speech and yet keep it sounding natural. It's hard!

Katherine Langrish

Tag lines

A tag line is what comes directly before or after a piece of dialogue, clarifying who said it, or how it was said. For instance, these are all tag lines:

'*I didn't know that,*' he said.

Sally replied, '*Well, you didn't ask, did you?*'

'*Typical,*' **John snapped.**

New writers sometimes feel that 'said' and 'asked' are boring words and that one should liven up tag lines whenever possible, but in fact the opposite is true. Look at what happens to the above piece of dialogue if it continues in such a vein:

'*I didn't know that,*' he said.

Sally replied, 'Well, you didn't ask, did you?'

'*Typical,*' John snapped.

'*What's that supposed to mean?*' she retorted.

'*Oh, just shut up!*' he interjected.

'*How dare you!*' she screeched.

'*Easily,*' he parried.

If your tag lines are many and varied, you run the risk of them becoming distracting to your reader. They become so fascinated by all that screeching and parrying that what your characters are actually saying to each other fades into the background. Your dialogue should sound so natural that readers are able to hear it as they read, as though they're there in the scene listening in. Anything that jolts them out of this illusion is to be avoided at all costs.

So don't despise 'said' and 'asked'; they're used so much because they work. Readers are so used to seeing these words that they're almost invisible, which allows your dialogue to spring into life without distraction. However, in a two-person exchange like the one above, you don't need to clarify who's speaking with every line; just remind your readers occasionally, so that they don't lose track. For instance:

'*I didn't know that,*' said John.

'*Well, you didn't ask, did you?*' said Sally.

'*Typical.*'

'*What's that supposed to mean?*'

'*Oh, just shut up!*' he said.

'*How dare you!*'

'*Easily.*'

If a third person jumped in at some point – Sally's mother, for instance – you would want to clarify who was speaking a bit more, though it might still be obvious in places. For instance:

'*I didn't know that,*' said John.

'*Well, you didn't ask, did you?*' said Sally.

'*Typical.*'

'*What's that supposed to mean?*'

'*Oh, just shut up!*' he said.

'John, you big oaf, how can you speak to your wife like that?' said Mrs Reinholdt.

'You shut up too!'

'Don't talk to my mother like that!' said Sally.

'Oh, I give up.'

Tag lines are only needed if there might be some uncertainty about who's speaking. You'll always want to use them at the start of an exchange to make things clear, but as the scene goes on, if it's obvious in context who's saying what, then you can leave the tag lines off altogether.

Character action

Tag lines aren't the only way to clarify your dialogue; you can add a bit of character action instead. This is an excellent way to make it clear who's speaking without having to say it explicitly, and also has the advantage of helping your reader see the scene more vividly. For instance:

'I didn't know that,' said John.

'Well, you didn't ask, did you?' Sally gazed at herself in the mirror, brushing her bright hair.

John blew out a breath between his teeth. 'Typical.'

She banged her hairbrush onto the dresser. 'What's that supposed to mean?'

'Oh, just shut up!'

'How dare you!'

'Easily.' Turning away, John propped his hands on the windowsill and stared out at the garden below.

A 'beat' or two of character action here and there can add a great deal of richness to your writing, and will bring a scene more sharply into focus for your readers. However, don't get so carried away with this technique that your scene begins to feel bogged down, with every spoken line accompanied by a paragraph of action. Keep the pace of your genre in mind, and keep things moving along.

Character-specific

Dialogue should always be **character-specific**. This means that your characters should sound like individuals, so that in general it's obvious who's talking from their speech alone. If all of your characters sound exactly alike, then you probably need to get to know them better – the exercises outlined in Chapter 02 should help.

In the example below, the dialogue is very 'samey', and might well mean that the author needs to rethink things a bit:

'Didn't anyone tell her? I mean, surely someone must have seen this coming,' said Pippa.

'No, I don't think so. Or maybe someone did, but no one quite had the courage,' said Lewis.

'Well, I think it's a disgrace. She shouldn't have just been left on her own like that.'

This is fairly natural-sounding dialogue, but it's so bland that you could practically swap the two characters about without noticing any difference. We need their personalities to be coming through more. For instance:

'But didn't anyone tell her? I mean – not to be rude, but – well, surely someone must have seen this coming,' said Pippa.

'Sure,' said Lewis. 'Why bother telling her though? Stupid cow! She got what she deserved, didn't she?'

'No, of course not! I think it's just a disgrace. She shouldn't have been left on her own; that's dreadful!'

Just from that brief exchange, you probably have a much better idea now of what sort of people Pippa and Lewis are. Get to know your characters so well that when they talk, it sounds like them and no other character. Though you'll of course use tag lines sometimes to keep things clear for your readers, make sure the reason they're needed isn't because your dialogue is so bland that no one could tell who was speaking otherwise.

Try this

Write a conflict between a teacher and a student, using only dialogue. Strive to make the two characters come vividly to life through their speech alone. It might help to think of two key words for each of them first. Avoid stereotypes, or else turn them upside down – for instance, what if the teacher is 'sulky and defensive', and the student is 'irritated and long-suffering'?

Try another conflict between a boss and an employee; a husband and wife; two adult friends. Note how strong dialogue doesn't need any tag lines or explanations – a reader can easily tell who's speaking and what emotions are being felt from dialogue alone.

Italics

Used sparingly, italics can be an effective means to emphasize a character's speech, but be careful with them. If used to excess, they can easily become irritating:

> '*Listen*, Horace, I will *never* forgive you, and that's *final*. Do you *understand? Never.*'

One feels that Horace cannot be blamed for whatever he did to the speaker; he was obviously driven to it. In contrast, taking the italics out makes the speech much stronger and angrier:

> 'Listen, Horace, I will never forgive you, and that's final. Do you understand? Never.'

Adding lots of italics doesn't strengthen your dialogue; it weakens it – your characters begin to sound hysterical and fake. If your dialogue is strong, your readers will add their own italics. Allow them the freedom to do this whenever possible; your dialogue will feel much more natural and real.

The exception to this might be if a character is meant to be gushingly over-dramatic:

> '*Hel-lo,* darlings! Oh, isn't this *wonderful*! I *never* thought we'd all be together again like *this*!'

While this might work for a particular character (though even here you don't want to overdo it; just use occasional italics to give us a flavour of his or her speech), in most situations you should only use italics as a last resort, if you're positive that a reader will misunderstand your meaning otherwise. In general, avoid them whenever possible. Put your words in place without adornment: the meanings behind your dialogue will shine through far more clearly with a bit of subtlety and restraint.

Slang

Though the goal of dialogue is to make your characters' speech sound real, be wary of using current slang, as it doesn't tend to stay current for very long. Fiction can easily feel dated by the use of words that no one's said for years, so it's usually better to give your characters' speech a natural flavour while using words that have stood the test of time.

However, if writing historical fiction, using slang from the era can help establish a particular time and bring your characters' dialogue to life. Do your research carefully, though; you don't want to sound like a foreigner using words he doesn't quite understand. Read novels and newspapers from the period, and watch films from the period if possible, so that you can use the language of the time in a natural-sounding way.

Dialect

A common problem for new writers striving to produce realistic dialogue is the issue of how to handle dialect (a particular vernacular or accent). The temptation, especially when you can hear your characters clearly, is to spell out exactly what you hear phonetically to your readers, so that your Geordie character who's about to go into town might say, 'I'm gannin doon the toon.'

The odd word or two in dialect is harmless enough; the difficulty comes when you try to reproduce longer speeches or conversations this way:

> *'Haway pet, I'm gannin doon the toon.'*
> *'Dee ye wanna meet in aboot two oo-az for a curry or summik?'*
> *'Aye, soonds reet canny.'*

For most people, this would be close to incomprehensible, not to mention extremely irritating to read. If readers are frowning at the page, sounding out strangely spelled words, they will have come out of the spell of your story with a bump and will not easily re-enter it. Instead, give your readers the flavour of a particular character's accent through their word choices and the rhythms of their sentences. For instance, you can easily tell the speaker's nationality here, without having to spell anything out phonetically:

> *Sure, and I won't be having it, so. Your mam'll kill me if she finds out.*

Strive for this sort of naturalness with your dialect, so that readers can hear your characters in their minds without being slowed down. Spell out the odd word if you really think it adds something, but keep this to a minimum. Pretend you're being fined £100 for each one, and budget yourself accordingly.

The same point holds true for a character who has a speech impediment. Nothing is more irritating to read than pages of speech where a character is stuttering on every word, or where their lisp is phonetically rendered with ruthless accuracy. Trust that your readers will remember the character's speech problem if you simply remind them of it occasionally.

Make sure it's needed

It can be easy to get carried away when your characters have sprung into life and are having long, animated conversations with each other, but remember that dialogue needs to have a definite purpose in your story. For instance, this sort of exchange could easily be cut:

> *'It's a beautiful day, isn't it?'*
> *'It certainly is. The sky's so blue!'*
> *'And isn't that warm breeze lovely?'*
> *'Spring's finally coming, all right. Look at the buds on that tree.'*
> *'I saw a bumblebee yesterday, too.'*
> *'Did you really?'*
> *'Yes, I really did. It was flying past my window.'*
> *'Oh, that's a sure sign of spring, too!'*
> *'I know, isn't it exciting?'*

If you find that your characters' conversation has become meandering and pointless (i.e. has nothing to do with your story or doesn't move things forward in any way), cut it. By the same token, don't be fooled into thinking that tension automatically means your dialogue is necessary. I've seen many manuscripts with pages of pointless bickering between characters:

> 'Look, Daz, I've already told you once!'
> 'Yeah? Well maybe you should tell me again.'
> 'Well, maybe I don't want to.'
> 'Maybe you should shut your mouth, then.'
> 'Who's gonna make me? You?'
> 'Maybe. Maybe I will. Then what will you do, huh?'
> 'No telling, is there? But you won't like it, I'll tell you that much.'
> 'Ooh, I'm scared. I'm shivering. See how scared I am?'
> 'Yeah, well, you _will_ be scared.'
> 'Scared of you? Don't make me laugh.'
> 'I'm not laughing. You won't be, either.'
> 'You're such a loser.'
> 'No, you are.'
> 'No, you.'
> 'You!'

There might well be tension here, but the two characters are essentially wittering now. Keep your writing sharp and focused: ask yourself what's needed for the scene to work, and then get rid of the rest. It's almost always the case that trimming down exchanges such as the above will strengthen their power tremendously:

> 'Look, Daz, I've already told you once!'
> 'Yeah? Well, maybe you should tell me again.'
> 'Maybe I don't want to.'
> 'Maybe you should just shut your mouth, then.'

Don't sneak in information your characters wouldn't say

You must always remain true to what your characters would actually say to each other. Don't try to 'sneak in' bits of exposition with unnatural dialogue such as this:

> 'Gurta! It's so good to see you! It must be, what, five years since the last time we saw each other?'

> '*Yes, Aman, that's right. It was just after that earthquake that destroyed our town, remember?*'
>
> '*Of course I do! And both of our families had gone missing, but you helped me find my mother … that was so nice of you.*'
>
> '*Don't mention it. I'm just glad I could return a favour. Don't forget, you helped me out that time I was wrongfully arrested when I was sixteen.*'

Never, ever do this. Dialogue such as the above sounds forced and fake, because both characters already know all of this perfectly well: the *only* reason they're coming out with these details is to give information to the reader. You have to be more subtle and truer to life than this. Get in your characters' minds and hearts, and don't try to force the conversation (or the action) to your own agenda. Remember that you don't have to reveal everything all at once. Readers like to wonder about things; it's what keeps them turning pages.

> '*Gurta, it's so good to see you … it's been so long.*'
>
> '*I know. Too long. I'm sorry for that, Aman, I just – I couldn't bear to see you again. I'm sorry; that sounds so blunt. It's nothing to do with you, it's just – *'
>
> '*It's OK, I understand. I guess I felt sort of the same way about you. Bad memories, and all.*'
>
> '*Yeah. Bad memories.*'

The reader is now much more intrigued than when the characters blurted out everything they knew about each other. Listen to your characters. Know who they are and how they would react in any situation, and remain true to it – you can't go far wrong if you do.

08

pacing

In this chapter you will learn:
- how to match your narrative pace to your story
- when to speed your narrative up
- when to slow your narrative down.

Pacing is your story's heartbeat: how quickly it moves at any given moment. Good stories seem to fly along during the exciting bits, then slow down so that a reader can catch his breath before picking him up and rushing forward again, all with a definite sense of direction and purpose. This is what blockbuster author Stephen King calls 'the gotta' factor: when readers feel that they 'gotta' keep reading to find out what happens next. If your readers stay up until three in the morning to finish your book because they can't bear to put it down, then you've got 'the gotta' factor – and your pacing is sure to be excellent.

Knowing your genre is essential for good pacing, as different types of fiction have widely varying conventions: for instance, historical fiction tends to spend a lot of time setting the scene, era and characters, while thrillers bring the action in quickly, and then keep it plummeting along. When writing teenage fiction, I'm always aware of 'beats' in my head, and I pay close attention to these, using only two or three beats for description before I return to what's happening with the story's action, or the main character. Become aware of the beats in your own genre, and use them.

Essentially, pacing is about craft: being in control of your talent rather than at the mercy of it. Several factors play a part:

- keeping tension present
- your handling of exposition
- knowing when to slow down
- knowing when to speed up – avoiding overwriting.

Tension

As discussed in Chapter 03, tension is the cornerstone of drama. Without tension in your scenes and overall storyline, readers are unlikely to find your story interesting.

A good rule in fiction is to up the stakes and make things as difficult as possible for your characters. Instead of giving them two weeks to save the world, give them two days – or two minutes if it's your climax. Think of your character's worst fear, and then make sure that's exactly what happens to them. While we sometimes tend to avoid tension in real life, the opposite should be true when crafting fiction.

> **Try this**
>
> Think of the absolute worst thing that could happen to your main character; the thing they dread the most. Is this thing currently happening in your story? If not, go back to your story plan and see if you can find a way to put it in. How does it change things? Does it make them more vital and exciting?

Exposition: keeping your cards close to your chest

New writers sometimes struggle with knowing when to disclose important information to their readers, and how much to disclose when they do. It can be tempting to tell readers all that you know about your story in the first chapter or two, but hold back. Your story's secrets are your most valuable possessions; don't give them away a moment before you have to. Readers love to be intrigued by mysteries – it's what keeps them flipping pages long into the night.

Dan Brown's mega-blockbuster novel *The Da Vinci Code* is an example of this, as it's crafted masterfully around a central secret that the reader is eager to find out about. With great skill, Brown takes readers through a trail of clues as his protagonists attempt to discover the truth about a secret society called the Priory of Sion. The reader is kept tensely involved as the various clues are found and deciphered, each taking us a few steps closer to the story's central revelation, but never giving so much away that the truth becomes clear a moment before Brown wants it to. Had Brown, perhaps in a prologue, included a scene taking place in Jesus's time where all was revealed, his book would not have been such a massive success.

This technique doesn't only apply to mysteries; it's used with great success in all genres. For instance, if your main character is guilt-stricken because she thinks she caused her father's death, this is just the sort of vital detail that you might want to hold back from telling your reader until the last possible moment. Instead of thinking, 'How soon can I get this information across?' think, 'How long can I hold back from revealing this?' Make a game of it; see how long you can hold out.

However, you don't want to simply hint endlessly through your character's thoughts and actions that something is wrong;

readers will quickly become irritated by this. Just as in *The Da Vinci Code*, think of your character's secret as a puzzle, and reveal it to your readers piece by piece. For instance, we might learn first that your main character has a dread of water; and then later that it's something to do with her father's death; and later still that it's because of the fishing trip they took together when he had a heart attack, and so on.

When you do give your reader a piece of information, keep show, don't tell in mind. Simply put your characters in place, and let them do the work themselves. For instance, a nosy uncle at a family gathering might make a comment that gives us a piece of the puzzle, or a concerned friend might press the main character to open her heart to her, which the main character is unable to completely do – though meanwhile we've received another puzzle piece. Hold back your most powerful card – exactly what happened in the boat, and why the main character blames herself – for as long as you possibly can. It might be that this detail doesn't come out until right at the story's end, as a result of your action climax. Or, perhaps it comes out a bit sooner, and facing her fears enables her to triumph.

Planning your story can help immensely with knowing when and where to reveal vital information. Work out your storyline with your revelations in mind, and know how they affect both the main character's emotional journey and the action plot.

The aspect of my writing that needed improving before getting published was the pacing – aiming to make sure that everything in the book either moves the plot on or informs the reader about the characters. I also needed to learn how to get straight into the action at the start of a book and how to feed in back-story over the first few chapters rather than following the temptation to put it all into the first few pages, thus slowing down the pace. Pacing becomes more automatic and instinctive with practice.

Linda Chapman

If you think your story doesn't have any secrets, look at it again – there's almost always a revelation that you can hold back with. Readers love to be hooked by a good mystery, to wonder what's going to be revealed. If you simply hand them your story's incidents on a silver platter, it's nowhere near as fun or involving for them.

Try this

Write a short story about a character who has a secret, and who's also physically trapped in some way, either with others or on her own. As your character strives to free herself from her predicament, show your reader that there is something else on her mind. Reveal her secret slowly, piece by piece, holding back its most vital part until the very end. Use interaction with other characters (if any) along with action events as catalysts for your revelations, taking care that they come out in a natural, unforced way. Notice how the different pieces of the secret, once revealed, might move the action story in a different direction.

When to slow down

In general, blockbuster fiction strives to plunge readers directly into action scenes and keep story events moving forward. However, you don't want your story to rattle along at such a breathless pace that it leaves readers confused or exhausted. I call this sort of writing 'skimming the surface', as it feels as if the author isn't delving deeply into what's happening, and is missing a great deal of potential depth and drama in the process.

Moments when you should particularly slow down include **dramatic events** and **sudden happenings**.

Dramatic events

If something important is happening to your characters – either emotionally or physically – you need to slow down so that readers can fully appreciate it. I often read manuscripts full of missed opportunities, where potentially wonderful dramatic moments are zipped through so quickly that their impact is lost.

For instance, the following passage isn't likely to make readers feel involved:

Xavier saw the finish line and ran harder than he had ever thought possible. He made it! He had won Olympic gold! The crowd cheered as they put the medal around his neck.

Dramatic moments in real life don't go by in a flash. Think of getting the big contract; being in a car crash; hearing about a loved one's death. Time seems to slow down at these moments as we become hyper-aware of the tiniest details. You don't want to go overboard here, but you do want to enter vividly into your scenes. Let readers savour the build-up as well as the payoff:

> *Xavier saw the finish line – a strip of blood-red against the grey track – and all sound dropped away, so that there was only the rhythmic pumping of his arms and legs, and his pulse slamming against his temples. He could see Pierre Buzet from the corner of his vision, a dark blur running at his elbow. Don't think. Keep going. His weak tendon shivered. No! Not now – he grit his jaw, pushed harder. Harder. The world faded into brilliant white, with only the finish line visible.*

> *And then he was through it, and the arena snapped into sharp focus. Thunder rumbled. No, it was the crowd – their voices a wall of sound roaring through him.*

If you think this is very similar to show, don't tell, you're right. In the case above, you could easily spend several pages on the race and its aftermath, taking us to the moment when Xavier is presented with the gold. By entering fully into your scenes, you'll get the most out of your dramatic moments.

Sudden happenings

Taking your time when something happens suddenly may sound like a contradiction, but see what happens when you don't give your reader a bit of a build-up:

> *Ursula and Bart picked their way through the blackened ruins of their home. 'I can't believe it,' said Ursula, hugging herself. 'Just yesterday, everything was so normal.'*

> *'I know.' Bart put an arm around her. 'Never mind, we'll get past this. We'll start again.'*

> *Suddenly the ceiling fell in on them.*

The action here is so abrupt that all tension is lost; the effect is humorous rather than dramatic. Remember, time slows down when something memorable happens. Use opportunities like this to build tension, and give your readers a chance to wonder what's going to happen. It makes for a far more involving read:

> *Ursula and Bart picked their way through the blackened ruins of their home. 'I can't believe it,' said Ursula, hugging herself. 'Just yesterday, everything was so normal.'*

'I know.' Bart put an arm around her. 'Never mind, we'll get past this.'

Ursula stiffened, peering upwards. 'What was that?'

Bart shook his head. 'I didn't hear anything.'

'No, there was a – a creaking noise, or something. I heard it – '

'You're imagining things, sweetheart – ' Bart broke off as a rainfall of scorched plaster pattered onto his shoulders. He took a step backwards, looking up at the ceiling.

'It doesn't look very stable, does it?' Ursula bit her finger.

Bart looked uncertain, but then he shrugged. 'I'm sure they wouldn't have let us in here if it wasn't safe.'

They both heard the creaking noise this time – a low sound, almost like the house moaning in pain. A piece of plaster the size of a dinner plate fell at their feet. Ursula jumped backwards, stumbling, and then there was a tearing crash and the world burst into falling debris and clouds of blackened plaster-smoke.

As rewritten, the scene is far more tense and convincing. We can believe in the ceiling falling down now; we've been prepared for it. Naturally, sometimes things will happen to your characters that they really have no preparation for – such as a car crash, for instance – but when this is the case, you want to slow things down to the level of hyper-reality the moment they occur, staying in your character's viewpoint (which may well be somewhat confused at first):

The car exploded into glass, and light, and sound. Something punched Margaret in the chest, pinning her to her seat. The motorway spun around and around, and Margaret knew she should brake, but her feet seemed disconnected, somehow; not working. She screamed and shut her eyes, and when the lurching motion finally stopped, she opened them. The dashboard was splattered with dots of red, and wind whistled through the car. Shattered glass covered her like icing sugar.

As a rule of thumb, when something is exciting or dramatic you should slow your pacing right down: readers are gripped, and they want details so that they can live what's happening moment by moment. And, when nothing of importance is happening, you should speed up and move on to the next point of action.

Strive for climaxes and lulls, with the story moving forward with every page.

Avoiding overwriting

Often, when new writers realize that they've merely been skimming the surface of their scenes and that there's a whole world of detail to be discovered in them, they'll get a bit overzealous and their work will become overwritten, full of unneeded information that doesn't add to their story. Aim for a happy medium. Give your reader enough time and details to live your scenes, but keep the 'beats' of story in mind and don't become bogged down.

Overwriting is an extremely common interim phase for new writers, so don't feel frustrated if you were at first told that your work was too skimpy, and now you're told it's too long and slow-moving. This is actually a positive sign, because it means you're seeing your scenes more vividly. You can always trim your work down, and it's better to have a lot of material to work with than thin scenes with no depth to them.

However, when you've become emotionally involved in your writing it can be difficult to step back from it and see what's needed and what's not. Often it *all* feels needed; it *all* feels important. Sadly, this is often just the author's delusion. My personal definition of overwriting is *writing that the author cares immensely about, but no one else does*. This should be your yardstick: if a particular passage were cut, would an objective reader sense a hole? Or would they not notice at all? In general, if you can cut something without leaving a gap behind, you should do so. If I'm uncertain whether to cut something or not, I'll take it out and see if I miss it upon re-reading. Nine times out of ten, it stays cut.

Planning your story out beforehand can help immensely here, as you can then clearly see the spine of your plot. When trimming your writing down, keep this spine firmly in mind. You need to be prepared to sacrifice passages and scenes (sometimes whole chapters and characters) that aren't vital to your storyline. This is called 'killing your darlings', and it can be a painful process at first – but with enough practice you become quite callous about it, and even begin to enjoy it.

What sort of darlings should you be eyeing up murderously?

Main character's inner voice

Though a strong main character is a plus in any novel, the danger for the author is that particularly vibrant main characters sometimes have a tendency to take over – commenting at length upon every piece of action, or regaling the reader with endless internal angst. For instance, in the following passage, you could easily trim more than half of the character's inner voice without losing any of the overall tone (and cutting down immensely on the annoyance factor):

> *I stared at her, unable to speak. She couldn't mean what I thought she meant, could she? She wasn't really dating Robert? The man I had loved for years? The cow! How dare she!*
>
> *'Tess, I – ' Beth faltered to a stop when she saw my face. My reddening, furious face. No doubt I looked like I was about to smack her one. And why not? My fingers itched with anticipation at the thought. I would have been totally entitled. My supposed best friend, stealing my boyfriend! How could she? Didn't she realize what she had done to me?*
>
> *'Shut up,' I told her. My voice trembled. 'Just shut up! I don't want to hear it.' I would have said more – in my mind, I did say more – but I couldn't. I just couldn't. I felt so betrayed. Beth and I had been friends for so long! I had trusted her completely. How could she do this to me, how?*

This is an example of a main character run amuck. While Tess might have a strong voice, at the moment it's buried under her endless internal wittering, taking away from the power of the scene.

It can be hard for an author to see this at times. When you hear your main character clearly in your mind, you often want to write down every word you hear them say – and if they're a strong character, they're going to be saying a great deal. Don't assume that their every word is golden and adding to your story. Look how much stronger the scene becomes simply from trimming Tess's voice down:

> *I stared at her, unable to speak. No. She couldn't mean it.*
>
> *'Tess, I – ' Beth faltered to a stop when she saw my face. No doubt I looked like I wanted to smack her one. My best friend! How could she do this to me?*

'Shut up,' I told her. My voice trembled. 'I don't want to hear it.'

We still have Tess's tone, but the pointless repetitions have been removed, leaving the passage much simpler and stronger. While we lose nothing of the scene's meaning, we've lost all of its dead weight: it now has room to breathe without clutter, and the reader isn't distracted by Tess's constant yakking.

Even with the most interesting of character voices, you can have too much of a good thing. The key is to develop strong main characters, let them talk all they want to in your first draft – and then go back with a red pen and look at what they're actually saying. Make sure that everything your character relates to us is needed. Very often, their inner voice will be rife with repeated points or obvious information that you can do away with.

If you find yourself doing too much explaining in first person I think you should stop and ask yourself why the character is doing this. Who's the implied audience/readership? Why is your character telling his or her story, and is it plausible for him or her to be doing so in this way?

Linda Newbery

Unneeded or overlong description

Though differences will apply here depending upon genre, in general it's best to keep description to a minimum. Paradoxically, the more you describe something, the harder it can be for a reader to visualize it, because they're having to juggle a myriad of details. I once read a manuscript that described the inside of an alien's spaceship in staggering detail, going on at length about the purple and red striped walls, the blue floor with green flashing flecks, the yellow ceiling with the golden light fixtures, the polka-dotted table with the fluorescent pink legs, the fuchsia kettle with the black cord, and on and on until it was a dizzying balancing act trying to keep everything straight in my mind. I quickly gave up, and decided on my own what the alien's ship looked like.

Your job as a writer is not to give your readers an exact photograph of what you see. Instead, strive to give them just a few pertinent, vivid details that will spark their own imaginations into life.

For instance, if you're describing a character's childhood home, you might say something like this:

> *The airy Georgian rooms were painted pale blue. Delicate white scallops encircled the ceiling, and golden cherubs flew high in every corner. His mother kept the silk drapes open, showing rolling gardens through the wavering glass. The furniture was scuffed at the edges, but still stately – muted wood and golden fabric, reflected softly in the polished cherry of the floors.*

This is really all you need; we now have a good idea of what sort of house it is and what it looks like. As described in the section on how to handle character description in Chapter 02, you can then give us other pieces of detail as the story goes on if needed, but again, the goal isn't to make your readers see exactly what you do. The house that your readers see may not be the same house that you imagine, and this is fine. It's now their house, that they've imagined based upon your creative touches, and they'll feel much more involved and interested as a result.

Try this

Describe a setting in lavish detail. Spend several pages on it, writing down every feature you can think of, until you're confident that this is an exact representation of the place you're trying to convey.

Now, go through and underline your favourite images: the pieces of detail that you think truly sum up the essence of the place. Using these favourite images, cut your description down to 150 words (about half of a double-spaced page). You'll probably have to choose between several of your favourite images to do this, which might seem impossible at first, but force yourself. Which ones most perfectly convey what you're trying to get across? Which are most essential? Play with your description, honing and polishing it until you get it just right.

Then, cut it down again. Try for 75 words this time. Look at the individual words that you can take out – for instance, instead of 'billowing white clouds', how about just 'billowing clouds'? Or instead of 'gleaming gold, expensive hinges', how about just 'gold hinges'? Experiment with how little you actually need to get your meaning across. You might be surprised.

Passages where nothing much happens

Think about the purpose of every line you write. What are you trying to accomplish? If it's primarily atmosphere or explanatory information, don't stop the action to delve into this; instead, try to bring in some action at the same time. As discussed in Chapter 03, you should make a scene perform several functions whenever possible. If you have a line or passage that doesn't add anything to your story, get rid of it. Prime candidates for this are often scenes that show characters travelling from one point to another, going to sleep, waking up, eating, and so on. Unless important exposition or dialogue is happening at the same time, such details can usually be cut with no loss at all.

It often helps to imagine your story as a film, and create/cut scenes accordingly. The next time you watch a film, notice how it's put together, scene by scene. When you feel your attention flagging in a film, it is often because the director has spent too much time on unnecessary information (such as characters driving their car to the shops). Normally, films don't show us every little thing a character does; they cut from scene to scene with *implied* action whenever possible, such as the following:

Interior shot, John's house

JOHN: Right, that's it. I'm going to go see Hattie.

CUT TO: Interior shot, Hattie's house.

JOHN: But why? I don't understand!

HATTIE: That's just the way it is, John.

No one watching the above on screen would be confused as to *how* John got to Hattie's house; this is information that doesn't add anything. Nor do we necessarily even need to see him ringing the doorbell, her letting him in, and so on. While films and novels are of course different media, envisaging your story in this way can be a very useful tool to pinpoint action that's unneeded.

> Fine writing is all well and good, but the question is whether it drives the story forward, while keeping the reader engaged — rather than sidetracking them (and you) away from the real action. With practice you'll be able to spot where you were treading water, waiting for inspiration, or where you've let the fancy stuff get away from you. Cut these parts out. Now, while you've got the time. Shorter is always better, and you don't want to realize that only when you've got the printed work in your hand.
>
> Michael Marshall Smith

I recently read a manuscript that had an excellent example of unneeded action. The story started with a grandfather telling his grandchild a story. He told a bit of the story, then decided it was getting late and the child should go to sleep. After extracting a promise that he could hear the rest of the story the next night, the child went to bed. While he was sleeping, his parents discussed the matter. They realized they weren't too sure what sort of story Gramps might tell if unsupervised, so they decided they'd better go along themselves the next night. The next chapter began with both child and parents present, as Gramps continued his story.

There was no logical reason for this break; it slowed the story down and didn't add anything to it. The author could have easily cut the entire first chapter and simply begun with chapter two, with parents and child both present during the storytelling. It then could have quickly been made obvious that the parents were there because they disapproved, adding another layer of depth to the scene and making it more involving.

Try this

Once you've written a few chapters of your blockbuster, read through it and find the point of tension in each of your scenes. Write a sentence noting it, along with the purpose of each scene. Keeping this in mind, look at your scenes again. Is there anything in them that has nothing to do with the scene's purpose? For instance, is there too much information about the weather, or a passage showing a character waking up and getting dressed, or a few lines of dialogue you could do without? Trim your scenes down as much as possible. Be completely heartless with yourself as you do so. See how late you can enter your scenes and how early you can leave them, while still giving us needed character and story information.

Information you have already told us. Resist the urge to 'sum up'

This can be a tempting sin to commit, because as a writer you're naturally concerned that your readers understand the ideas you're trying to get across. Be firm with yourself and resist. If you've shown your readers every detail of a thrilling bank heist, there's no reason for your thieves to have this sort of conversation a few pages later:

> *'Hurrah!' said Penny. 'We did it! We've got our million!'*
>
> *'Too bad we has to shoot that guard, though,' said Frank.*
>
> *'Don't blame yourself. We couldn't let him call the cops, could we?.'*

This dialogue's only purpose is that the author is afraid you might not have noticed that the thieves got their million and that a guard was shot during the robbery. If the original scene is strong enough, there is no way that this could be the case. You might argue that this dialogue gives character information, but readers should find out about your characters while they're doing something new that moves the story forward, rather than stopping to discuss an event we already know about.

Too much recapping quickly becomes tedious, and can even feel condescending to your readers. Write to the highest intelligence of your audience. Show them something once in a vital, vivid way, and then trust that they'll remember it. Avoid recap unless a significant amount of time has passed, and then keep it as brief as possible.

But it's so well-written!

Though it can be painful to cut passages you think are wonderful, never keep something in just because it's well-written and you like it. If you're a professional writer, everything you write needs to be well-written. When a sequence is weighing down your story for one of the reasons listed above, the fact that it may be well-written is beside the point: if it doesn't add to your story, it has to go.

Cuts don't have to be big

Finally, keep in mind that minor cuts can, cumulatively, make just as big an impact as major ones. I've seen overwritten manuscripts that went on just a touch too long per paragraph, with one or two unneeded sentences. The overall impact weighed the story down significantly. Simply cutting an unneeded word or two can make a real difference to an individual line. So first look at the big, obvious cuts – scenes, chapters, characters – and then look at your work paragraph by paragraph, line by line, and consider what smaller cuts you can make, too. Remember, if you can do without something – be it a word, a sentence, a paragraph, a scene or a chapter – you should.

Questions to ask yourself

- What's the purpose of this line/passage?
- Does it support my story arc, or have nothing to do with it?
- Is there another line/passage that fulfils this same purpose?
- If I took it out, would it leave a hole?

> The main thing that needed improving was overwriting – both before and after my first book was published, and possibly still! For a long time I knew there was something I didn't like about my writing, but couldn't identify what it was. Now I do know, and spend a long time reading and rereading my work, and – very importantly – cutting.
>
> Linda Newbery

09
rewriting and self-editing

In this chapter you will learn:
- how to assess your first draft
- about the value of other people's opinions
- what to do with feedback once you have it.

The key to finishing a first draft is to keep looking forward: don't read over what you've done so far, or else you'll be tempted to start taking the story apart, and then find yourself reworking the same few chapters over and over. Just keep your head down, focus on the scene at hand, and stick to your writing goals. Your novel will grow by leaps and bounds, and you'll be done in what seems like no time.

If this is the first time you've ever completed a novel-length draft, you should feel immensely pleased with yourself. Aside from the thrill of actually completing a story for the first time, the best thing about finishing this first draft is breaking the psychological barrier. You know now that you *can* write a book, and having done it once, you can do it again. You're on your way.

However, ten minutes after you finish your novel is not the time to trust your own judgement about the story's strengths and weaknesses. At this moment, every word you wrote will seem golden to you – and that's how it should be. You've just accomplished something momentous.

Once you've had a good initial gloat, put your book firmly away for now and celebrate your accomplishment. I have a tradition of celebrating my first drafts with champagne, but if champagne isn't your thing, develop your own tradition. Celebrate in some way that makes you happy and marks the occasion of your accomplishment properly.

Don't peek

Is your book tucked away someplace where you can't stumble across it by accident? Good. Leave it there for at least three weeks. The temptation to look through it and start tweaking will be almost unbearable, but ignore it. You need some distance on your story to be able to view it objectively, and time is the only way you'll achieve that.

Instead of twiddling your thumbs and going mad during this time, start developing another story. The book you've just finished is not the only book you'll ever write, so don't act as though it is. Starting work on something else will help put things greatly in perspective when you finally allow yourself to read through your draft.

Reading through your draft

Once the three weeks are up, turn the phone off and send your family out for the day so you won't be disturbed. Get a cup of coffee or a glass of wine, make yourself comfortable, and sit down to read through your draft. Having got a bit of distance on it, you'll be in a far better position to see what sort of story you've written and where its problem areas lie (and there are sure to be some; no first draft is perfect). As you read, try to pretend that your manuscript was written by someone else.

Be aware that it's very common for authors to unconsciously fill in any gaps in a story, when a completely objective reader would just be confused at what isn't there. Try not to do this. Read actively, noticing what's there and what's not. Are your characters' motivations shown to your readers? Are there any plot-holes? And, notice how you react to the story on a visceral level. Does the pace seem as though it's dragging anywhere? Do you like the main character and feel involved in her problem? Write down your thoughts as you go: what you think is working, what isn't, and what you'd like to change.

Reading through your own work can be both exhilarating and uncomfortable. You might be thrilled at the brilliance of some of your passages; others might fill you with despair at how rubbish they are. Keep reading through these emotions, and try not to take them too seriously. You're naturally very emotionally involved in your story, but the job at hand is simply to read through it and ask yourself questions. Again, keep in mind that no first draft is going to be perfect.

After your initial read-through, you might know immediately what some of the book's issues are, and exactly how you want to address them. Or you might just feel confused at this point. Maybe you think some parts of the book are good, but others you're not sure about. Either way, your writer's support system (discussed in Chapter 01) is vital now.

Don't write in a vacuum

Authors aren't always the best judges of their work. Though you'll get much better at spotting problem areas in your drafts with practice, there are always going to be things you might miss (sometimes major ones). *Writers need readers.* Your goal as a writer is to communicate your story effectively, and you can't know if you've accomplished this until you show your draft to someone.

This can seem very daunting, particularly if you've never shared your work with anyone before, so choose your readers carefully. Ideally, you'll have a writing buddy or two whose opinions you can trust. If not, maybe you're a member of a writing group (either online or off), and could show your novel to a few members with whom you feel in tune. A good reader doesn't have to be a writer, though. If you know someone who reads a great deal in your chosen genre, they might be an excellent person to show your work to for comments.

Or, perhaps you've made a good contact through a writing course or conference that you could use. This isn't the time to show your work to agents and editors, but if you've met a professional writer who showed an interest in your work, you might politely approach them and ask if they'd read a chapter or two (don't ask them to read the whole thing unless they offer). Most writers are very generous, and you might get lucky – but don't be annoyed if they say no.

> I was interviewing Richard Adams for the *Times Ed* (the paperback of *Watership Down* had recently come out and he was making serious money). At the end of the evening, I rather hesitantly admitted that I had written a children's book myself and when he drove me home he insisted on my going in and fetching the manuscript for him to read. Wasn't that kind and above and beyond the call of duty?
>
> Mary Hoffman

Friends and family members aren't always the best readers. Sometimes they're so impressed that you've written a complete manuscript that this blinds them somewhat, not to mention that they care about you and don't want to hurt your feelings with negative feedback. However, there are exceptions, and if you have no one else to read your work, you can 'train' friends and family to think critically about what you show them. Don't be content with their exclamations about your genius and the impossibility of improving a single word. Instead, ask them specific questions about your characters, the storyline, where they found their attention flagging, what they liked and disliked. With a bit of delving you should have an idea of what they really think and what areas need strengthening.

There's also the option of going to a professional literary consultancy, where you pay a fee to have a professional writer or editor read your work. You'll then receive a written report that discusses the story's strengths and weaknesses in detail, with suggestions for how you can improve it. Though authors in many different situations find this a valuable service, it's probably particularly valuable for those who don't have a support system in place and are unsure of the way forward. If this is your situation then purchasing professional feedback is something you might wish to consider.

If you've written a children's book, by all means show it to children (as well as adult readers) for their comments, though you'll probably get a more unbiased response if they don't know you're the author. However, beware of taking your work into classrooms and reading it aloud. New authors sometimes think that an enthusiastic response from a classroom means that they have a children's blockbuster on their hands. Keep in mind that you can't go along with your manuscript to read it to agents and publishers: your words must stand on their own, without the help of your dramatic inflections or tone of voice.

The art of receiving feedback

Receiving feedback on your work for the first time can sometimes be an uncomfortable experience. You've put heart and soul into your writing, and any criticism of it, no matter how gently put, can feel very personal. Though it can be difficult, you need to listen to your reader's response without argument, and accept that their comments are a valid opinion whether you agree with them or not.

That's not to say that you shouldn't ask questions, or clarify a point that you don't understand. Feedback should ideally be a two-way process, with author and reader kicking ideas around and discussing what works and what doesn't. In fact, it can often be an exhilarating experience, particularly if the issues raised by your reader resonate with you, and you realize that the way forward isn't so murky after all. This is the best possible scenario, and can be a massive relief when you've been worried about what to do next.

Sometimes, though, you may be unsure what you think of the problem areas targeted by your reader. Perhaps she's told you that your pacing is too slow when you think it's fine, or that she hates your beloved main character and thinks you should make radical changes to his personality. Should you automatically take her advice? The key here is to *trust your instincts*. Writing is a hugely subjective business. There might indeed be a particular problem that needs addressing, but it might also be that your reader isn't on your wavelength and isn't 'getting' your story.

However, even if your reader is a tried and trusted one, you should never make a change simply because she said you should, or a change that you're unsure about. You can't implant someone else's ideas onto your story and expect them to succeed. They have to go through *your* creative process first, so that they become your own ideas, with your own imaginative touches and sense of excitement about them. If this doesn't happen, it's best to look for another way forward.

Be aware that you will need to go through about four drafts before it's completely right. And don't reject advice out of misplaced vanity. Sometimes others really do know best. However, if your whole being recoils from a suggestion, don't follow it.

Adele Geras

A particular author comes to mind who wrote a children's novel with an awkward mix of rollicking humour and grim darkness. I advised him that this was a tricky combination to pull off, and that he should focus on one tone or the other. He went away for several months, and when I read his manuscript again, I saw that he had taken on board some of my suggestions to do with his plot, disregarded others – and kept the humorous/dark tone. He told me that he was convinced it could work, and so instead of focusing on one or the other as I had suggested, he had instead worked at balancing them more smoothly together.

It worked brilliantly, and I saw immediately that he had been right to trust his instincts (he's since gone on to get a publishing contract). However, I had also been right, as his original tone hadn't worked as it was. This is the key to successfully implementing feedback: don't just do what someone else tells you to. Accept that there might be a problem, but look for ways to solve it that feel right to you.

If ten Russians tell you you're drunk...

If possible, you should show your work to more than one person, so that you receive different perspectives on your story. Often, one reader will pick up on something that another one missed, or your readers will all agree on a certain point. While you should trust your instincts, you do need to pay serious attention to consensus opinion. If every person you show your story to reports that they didn't understand a particular plot twist, then there's a problem with it that needs to be addressed, no matter how attached to it you are. As my colleague Jen Upton often points out during our workshop courses, 'If ten Russians tell you you're drunk, lie down.'

> I tended to rush endings; I know because different people reading my work made the same point. So it was a matter of remembering that, and pacing myself. Planning my plots in some detail helped.
>
> Kate Long

What if my readers say different things?

This can be a very confusing situation for a writer. One reader tells you that he loves one of your plots twists but hates your main character, while another reader says he saw the plot twist coming from a mile away, but your main character is fabulous. What are you supposed to make of that?

If your readers say wildly divergent things, then the deciding vote is down to you. Consider carefully what has been said. Is there really a problem there? Is there anything you think you should change? Take your time, and do what feels right to you. It's also important to keep in mind that a problem may have several solutions, and there's probably no *one* thing that you must do to fix it. Look for the underlying problem that's been flagged, rather than focusing on proposed solutions if you're unsure about them.

As an example, my agent Caroline Sheldon once told me about an author whose manuscript she read. Caroline felt that one of the characters didn't work, and suggested that the author cut him from the story. The author wasn't sure what he felt about this, and showed his book to someone else. The second reader gave the opposite advice: she felt that the character should be fleshed out and given a larger role. The author went back to Caroline in despair: 'What do I do? You've said totally different things!'

Caroline pointed out that in fact, she and the second reader were in complete agreement: there was a problem with this particular character. How the author chose to deal with this problem – either cutting the character out or building him up – was up to him.

Take your time and think it through

When you first receive feedback, it can be very tempting to dive back into your story and start making changes to it immediately. Stop! You should take at least several weeks before you change a single word. I've read a lot of manuscripts after the author has revised them on the back of comments, and my heart always sinks when the author reports within a matter of weeks that they've finished their next draft. Sometimes this really is all the work that's needed, but more often the rewrite will feel rushed, with all of the original problem areas still intact despite surface cosmetic changes.

> Writing the first draft is the fun bit. Reworking is where the hard graft comes in, but reworking is the process that makes or breaks a book so it can't be skipped. Never send out a manuscript which you feel could benefit from a bit more work. If you feel that, then so will the editor/reader and it's more likely to get rejected.
>
> Malorie Blackman

The most successful rewrites tend to be those where the author has given herself time to do a great deal of thinking, and has delved deeply into the roots of problem areas instead of blindly following suggestions. You need to give yourself the creative space to thoroughly consider any new ideas, and see where they take you. Go for long walks, mull over everything that's been said, scribble ideas down in your writer's notebook. It might help to get your notecards out again, or to write a new synopsis to see how the changes fit on a story arc. Most importantly, take your time and be sure that any changes you make feel right to you, rather than making hasty changes that will be difficult to undo later.

How many drafts?

It's not unusual to have to make substantive changes to your first draft, so be prepared for this, and don't despair if this turns out to be the case. Even with careful planning beforehand, you just can't always know whether a particular character or storyline will work until it's actually written. The important thing is that you now have a complete draft in place: raw material that you can shape and play with.

Whether the changes facing you are great or small, you're almost certainly looking at the necessity of a second draft, and probably even a draft or two after that. By 'draft', I mean a version of your story where you're still experimenting somewhat – making changes, sometimes significant ones, to see if they work. However, with each draft you do, the choices facing you should narrow as the way forward becomes clearer. If each draft you tackle instead seems to open up a morass of possibilities that takes you further away from your original intention, you need to stop and consider. It might be that you should return to the planning stage to ensure that things aren't getting out of hand.

> When I've finished a story I'll type it all on to the computer, editing as I go. Then I read it all again and think it's horrible, and get very depressed. Eventually, after a lot of fiddling, it's sort of all right, but the best I can do; and that's when I send it off to the publisher.
>
> Philip Pullman

How many drafts should you do before submitting your blockbuster to an agent? There's no single answer that will fit every manuscript. For some writers, two or three drafts and a polish are plenty; others might be looking at ten drafts or more. The key is to know when the book is as good as you can make it at this point in time. You should ask yourself the following before you consider submitting:

- Does your novel feel like a good, solid piece of work to you?
- When you read through it using the techniques described in Chapters 03 (structure), 06 (writing style) and 08 (pacing), do you find that you have few, if any, corrections to make?
- Do you have an interesting main character with an involving problem? Are your characters real people to you?

- Does the storyline have a definite arc, with strong emotional and action plots?
- Have you addressed all of those niggling little issues that you were aware of but hoping no one else would notice? (If not, address them before submission. Never bury your head in the sand over these things; they could be the difference between being published and not being published.)
- Do readers who have read your novel before enthuse about how well your changes work, and how smoothly it reads now?
- Do readers seeing it for the first time have only minimal comments (and lots of praise)?
- Finally, have you given the manuscript a good copy-edit and polish, making sure that it looks neat and professional, with no misspelled words or grammatical errors?

If the answer to all of the above is 'yes', then congratulations – you're ready to go to part two of this book and learn how to submit your work.

When should you set a story aside?

In general, my feeling is that you shouldn't spend more than two years on any particular project. You're growing and changing all the time as a writer, and if you cling to one particular novel, rewriting it over and over again, you're likely to hold yourself back. Additionally, stories that have been extensively reworked over a period of years often lose any sense of freshness that they once had. If you haven't made your story as good as you can make it after two years, it's probably best to put it aside and move on to something new.

New writers often react to this idea with horror: 'But I'll have wasted all that time I spent on it!' Time spent writing is never a waste. Just because a particular book doesn't get published doesn't mean that it hasn't helped further you along the path of your career. Often you'll find that your writing skills have progressed enormously during your struggles on a particular novel, even if the story in question never quite comes together. When you put it aside and begin something new, you might be amazed to find that your work has taken a quantum leap forward in quality and self-confidence. (And, you might return to your earlier novel at a later stage when your skills are more solid, and find that you can turn it into something publishable.)

Remember that almost every published author has a few journeyman manuscripts tucked away, and that these authors might not have got published if they hadn't set their earlier, flawed works aside and started writing something else. So if you've given a particular novel your best shot, don't be afraid to put it aside. Don't keep your writing stuck in the past – let it grow and change along with you.

10

the A–Z of genres

In this chapter you will learn:
- the basic conventions of the major blockbusting genres.

First, a word of warning: don't depend on this chapter when writing your blockbuster. You need to be very familiar with the genre in which you choose to write, and a guide such as this one can't begin to replace detailed personal knowledge of titles, conventions and trends. Do your research! There are also excellent books and websites that focus specifically on particular genres; some of these are listed in 'Taking it further'. However, just to give you an idea of what sort of genres (and sub-genres) are out there, here's a quick guide.

Children's

Children's fiction is fiction aimed primarily at children. It's an exciting, burgeoning market, with many new writers seeing blockbuster possibilities in the wake of the Harry Potter phenomenon. And, certainly at the older end of the children's market, these titles aren't read only by children: numerous adults have become aware of the excellent fiction to be found here, which has led to the new genre of crossover fiction (see below).

Children's fiction is broken down into several categories relating to the target age of the child. Roughly, you have the following.

Picture books

Normally meant to be read to children of ages three to seven by their parents. Pictures and text work equally together to tell a story. Picture books normally consist of twelve two-page spreads, which must be taken into account when writing them. Don't attempt to draw the pictures yourself or to have a friend do it unless you or they are a professional illustrator. Publishers prefer to choose illustrators from their own 'stable'. (While this book isn't aimed at picture book writers – which is a very specialized type of writing – it's good to know generally the format for this genre.)

Younger fiction/early readers

These are titles targeted at children just beginning to read on their own, roughly aged five to eight, and are often illustrated or broken down into easily digestible chapters. There's a broad range of word count/fluency expectation to this genre, with particular publishers' lists varying widely (and changing from year to year, so that research is vital).

Junior/middle readers

Aimed at children from about eight to twelve. At the time of writing, this is the largest and most popular area of children's fiction, with a large number of new titles being brought out every month. Subject matter can be almost anything; there are sub-genres of real-life fiction, historical, fantasy and science fiction. Currently, this is a difficult market to break into, with publishers being extremely discriminating.

Teenage/young adult

Aimed at older readers, aged about thirteen and upwards. Deals with issues in a more mature, graphic way than in junior fiction, though the subject matter might often be the same. Again, there are sub-genres of real-life fiction, historical, fantasy and science fiction.

Crossover

This is children's fiction that also appeals widely to adults, and is the stuff blockbusters are made of. Crossovers tend to be marketed towards both audiences simultaneously, sometimes with different front covers. These titles often begin life as children's fiction, and only later become crossover successes once 'discovered' by an older audience. Though they can be hugely popular, I wouldn't advise setting out to write a crossover – they occur more by happenstance than plan.

Chick-lit

As a broad definition, this is feel-good fiction (i.e. it almost always has a happy ending) by women for women, and tends to centre on attractive, interesting heroines in their twenties and thirties. Whether in the first or third person, the tone is normally personal and humorous, with a sharp contemporary slant. The subject matter focuses on timeless concerns such as family, friendship and career, with romance usually playing a major role.

Crime

Crime fiction, as you might expect, focuses on crimes: the motives of the criminals who commit them, and their ultimate detection. Often (though not always) the identity of the criminal is kept hidden from the reader until the very end: they must strive, along with the character attempting to solve the crime, to deduce the culprit through the clues placed in the story. Crime fiction is hugely popular and widely varied, but its main sub-genres include:

- capers
- classic whodunnit
- cosy
- crime/detective
- historical mystery
- noir
- police procedural
- private eye.

Fantasy

Along with science fiction, fantasy is known as 'speculative' fiction – fiction that speculates about other worlds. Broadly, fantasy focuses on worlds that, by our current scientific knowledge, could never exist: places where you might have magic, mythical creatures, humans with the power of flight, and so on. However, this is only a rough definition. Fantasy is an extremely vibrant and wide-ranging genre, with many variations on the basic 'worlds that couldn't exist' theme. A partial list of sub-genres includes:

- Arthurian fantasy
- comic fantasy
- dark fantasy
- epic fantasy
- heroic fantasy
- high fantasy
- magic realism
- modern fantasy
- sword and sorcery.

Historical

Historical fiction is fiction that's set in a specific time in the past: usually at least 50 years prior to the book's publication, or a time that pre-dates the life of the author. While some of the characters might be wholly fictional, the cast will probably also include real people from the time period. Historical fiction is typically a serious attempt to bring a particular time, person(s) and/or episode to life for its readers, and normally includes extensive research to this end. However, liberties might sometimes be taken in the name of fiction. Sub-genres include:

- alternate histories
- historical fantasy
- historical mystery
- pseudo histories
- time-slip.

Horror

As a catch-all definition, horror generally strives to frighten or unsettle its readers. It might include supernatural elements such as ghosts, werewolves and vampires, or it might seek to disturb simply through the weirdness of its concept. Horror isn't easily pigeon-holed, as it often crosses genres: for instance, you might have horror in a science fiction setting, or in a historical one. Deciding where such titles ultimately belong comes down to where the publisher thinks they'll sell the best, based on the author's past titles or current marketing trends. Horror sub-genres include:

- cutting edge
- dark fiction
- erotic horror
- extreme
- gothic
- noir
- psychological
- supernatural.

Lad-lit

Similar to chick-lit, lad-lit is sharp, contemporary fiction that focuses on modern men and their concerns in a humorous way.

Mainstream

This is something of a catch-all genre, and generally means a work that the publishers think will have a wide commercial appeal. Mainstream novels tend to fall outside of more specific genres; they commonly, though not always, focus on universal concerns in a real-life setting.

Romance

A hugely popular genre, romance focuses on two main characters who fall in love, and who then must struggle to maintain that love throughout difficult circumstances that threaten to drive them apart. This genre traditionally has a happy, emotionally satisfying ending: its readers want to experience the highs and lows of a relationship through strong, appealing characters, but to know that love will prevail in the end. While the above guidelines hold true for all romantic fiction, the stories themselves may vary widely in length and explicitness depending upon which publisher's list the title is on. Romance sub-genres include:

- contemporary
- erotic
- family saga
- fantasy
- futuristic
- historical
- paranormal
- regency
- romantic
- time-travel
- western.

Science fiction

Along with fantasy, science fiction is known as 'speculative' fiction – fiction that speculates about other worlds. Broadly, science fiction focuses on worlds that might, given our current scientific knowledge, either exist now or exist someday, though we don't currently have first-hand knowledge of them. Common themes are space travel, alternate realities and contact with alien worlds. However, like fantasy, science fiction is a vibrant and wide-ranging genre, with almost limitless variations on the basic 'worlds that might be' definition. A partial list of sub-genres includes:

- aliens
- alternate reality
- classic
- cyber punk
- dystopia
- frontier
- hard science fiction
- lost worlds
- other worlds
- post-apocalypse
- space opera
- space travel
- time travel
- utopia.

Thriller

Though they commonly focus on a crime of some description, thrillers are distinct from crime novels, as their main goal is to stimulate the reader through their fast pace and high levels of suspense and action. While generally somewhat 'light' reads, thrillers tend to be very well constructed, and have a wide following. Some sub-genres include:

- action-adventure
- conspiracy thriller
- espionage
- forensic thriller

- legal thriller
- medical thriller
- military thriller
- political thriller
- religious thriller
- romantic suspense
- techno-thriller.

Western

Though normally set in the 1800s in the American West, westerns are distinct in tone from historical fiction. They're commonly fast-moving, and often focus on the theme of a lone man struggling against injustice. Other common themes include taming the frontier, and the codes of honour that existed among the settlers who did so. There is often a central character (or group of characters) somewhat outside of society: a loner or anti-hero. Westerns are commonly moral tales, with good prevailing over evil. Once hugely popular, westerns have been declining in popularity in recent years, though author Larry McMurtry's exploration of this genre has helped to revive it.

Women's

Women's fiction, broadly, is fiction that's thought to appeal more to women than to men. It's a mainstream term, and often includes novels centring upon relationships, career, family and the home (though women's novels can also range far wider than these concerns). Genres that might fall within this general category include **chick-lit** and **romance**.

part

two
submitting a blockbuster,
getting an agent and
being published

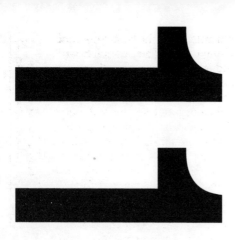

the common
sense approach
to submitting

In this chapter you will learn:
- what an agent can do for you
- how to submit your work in a professional way
- how to turn rejection into a positive.

An effective agent can play a vital role, both in launching and then helping to establish your writing career. Their contacts and knowledge of the publishing industry often make them an invaluable help to authors. They'll send your work out to publishers, targeting those who they know are likely to enjoy it, and if you get a contract they're skilled negotiators who will fight to get you the best possible deal. A good agent will also help steer and guide your career, liaising with your publisher for you when needed and giving you sound advice on foreign deals, subsidiary rights, and other areas. In addition, some agents are talented editors, and can give pertinent feedback on your manuscripts.

An agent will advise an author in the early stages of a book's life, before submission to publishers. Once the publisher has acquired the book, then the editor takes over that role. The agent will advise on future ideas and their potential.

Catherine Clarke, Felicity Bryan Literary Agency

An agent is normally with you for as long as you want them to represent you, whereas there's often a higher turnover in editorial departments, with editors getting promoted or moving to a different publishing house. (Or, you as an author might move to a different publisher.) Agents are in it for the long term, and can represent a welcome stability that authors don't always have otherwise. Though you may not want to part with 10–15% of everything that your book makes, a productive agent will work hard for their percentage, and more than earn their keep.

While it's not always essential to have an agent, for most writers it's the first step, as many publishers no longer look at unsolicited material (material that comes to them directly from authors). It's therefore important to know how to submit your work with confidence and professionalism, so that they'll sit up and take notice. (If you do choose to submit your work directly to publishers, the principles outlined in this chapter are much the same whether you're submitting to agents or editors.)

It's good to know that:

- agents (and editors) want to find new talent
- once you know how, submitting your work can be straightforward

- if your manuscript is not up to standard it's likely to be rejected
- luck and timing play important roles, so don't fall at the first hurdle.

Do your research

While it can be tempting to send a copy of your manuscript to every agent in the *Writers' and Artists' Yearbook* (published annually by A&C Black; see 'Taking it further'), a bit of research and careful targeting will make the process less time-consuming, and will normally reap far better results.

For an agent to take you on, they need to love your work and think they can sell it. You therefore need to be aware of the sort of list they handle, and whether your type of fiction is likely to be of interest. Study the *Writers' and Artists' Yearbook* before you submit, and note the sorts of fiction that various agents handle. It's no good sending your fantasy novel to an agent who exclusively deals with crime fiction. Most agents have websites, which will give you an idea of the authors they already represent and the feel of the agency. (Remember that a small agency can be just as powerful, with all the necessary contacts, as a larger agency.)

Use the contacts that you've been developing. For instance, you might meet an agent who handles your sort of fiction at a writers' conference, or hear of one through your writers' group. You might read an interview with or attend a talk by an agent, which could be a perfect hook to contact them. How flattering and pertinent it would be, for example, if you wrote in your cover letter, 'I read an interview in the recent issue of *Writers' Forum* where you said were looking to commission thriller writers. I wonder if my novel, *Killer on the Loose,* might be of interest?'

Compile a list of the particular agents you think would be perfect to handle your work, and then choose the top two or three for your first round of submissions. (While it's true that some agents prefer exclusive submissions, targeting two or three at a time means you're not limiting your chances and you're not wasting anyone's time.) Keep in mind that each agent is different. They all have their preferred means of receiving submissions, so for your blockbuster to receive its best possible chance, you need to know what these are. Call the agency to check the name of the person you're submitting to, and ask for the preferred submission procedure.

From the moment someone in the agency picks up the phone, be organized and professional. You never know to whom you might be speaking: it may be the receptionist – some are would-be agents whose job may also be to process the submissions pile – or it might be the agent, so be prepared to answer questions about your manuscript and who you are. It's helpful to have your synopsis or paragraph blurb (see sections later in this chapter for more detail) and covering letter to hand, (although avoid reading these out verbatim), as you may find that your mind goes blank when an agent asks the first question about your book. Most agents and assistants are extremely busy so don't feel brushed off if the call ends sooner than you might like; remember, you're primarily checking the contact name and submission procedure at this stage.

If you do speak to the agent they will have a good idea if a story is right for them so respect their decision – and try not to take it personally if they decline to see your submission package. On the other hand, they may love the sound of your story and ask you to send some sample material through immediately.

If you're finding it hard to get the information you require, try not to feel frustrated. Instead, try another avenue. Write a short email or letter. Attach your submission letter, synopsis and sample chapters and make it easy for the agent to get in touch with you in case they want to see more. Never email the whole manuscript unless an agent requests it.

129
the common sense
approach to submitting
11

I began by submitting a few chapters to a handful of different agents and got the usual rejections. So I started another novel, but also booked to go to a writers' conference: not because I thought it would work wonders, but to get a sense of the industry and maybe some new ideas. I entered the first few pages of my novel into a competition there, won first prize and the publisher that judged the competition signed me for *Old School Ties* – which came out about 20 months after I wrote that opening line.

Kate Harrison

Your submission package

Your submission package should consist of your submission letter, a synopsis, and your first three chapters. Don't send other chapters from further along in the story, even if you think these are your best – your manuscript should be strong throughout. Also include a stamped addressed jiffy bag if you need your material returned. Make sure it has stamps on it, and not the white stickers with the day's date that the Post Office will try to issue, as these will go out of date almost immediately.

Submission letter

Your submission letter is usually an agent's first impression of you, and it's important that this impression is a professional one. Agents are not only looking at your work; they're also trying to get a sense of who you are: would they like to work with you as a client, or would you be difficult to deal with? Keep your letter short, simple and contemporary; aim to get the agent reading your chapters as quickly as possible. Avoid weird fonts – use Times New Roman size 12 or something similar – and use black ink. Don't forget to include your contact details: name, address, phone and email.

Your submission letter should be addressed to the particular agent who you'd like to handle your work. Make sure you have the correct spelling of the agent's name, and don't address them by their first name or a nickname; this can be an instant turn-off.

> Make sure your letter is addressed to the right person – if an author can't get that piece of research correct, what does it say about the rest of the work?
>
> Carole Matthews

In your first few lines, introduce the book and say that you're looking for representation. You'll need to summarize your novel in a way that encapsulates the story, setting, genre and word length: 'As discussed, I am looking for representation for my rags-to-riches novel set in nineteenth-century England and New York, *The Millkeeper*, 120,000 words.' For **children's writers** the audience/age group you're aiming your story at also needs to be specified, for instance: '*Spiral World* is a fantasy novel for middle readers, 40,000 words.'

You should also let them know a bit about yourself, and whether you've been published before. If you have, let them know the genre, title of the book, the publisher and the year it was published. If it was self-published say so. Also list any awards or competitions that you've won or been shortlisted for, though make sure these are recognized ones that the agent is likely to have heard of.

Is there something about you that makes you particularly suitable to have written a novel in your genre? If you're a teacher and you write for children, or you're a scientist and you have a sci-fi novel, then this is all related information, as is anything that might show you in an interesting light. Perhaps you started writing in your late 80s (this is a great publicity hook if your first novel turns out to be a blockbuster); or perhaps you live in a caravan in the Outer Hebrides. And, if there's anything about you that might add to your writing credentials – for instance, perhaps you're a TV producer or journalist – then by all means mention it.

However, you don't have to be exotic or unusual, so don't worry if you have nothing colourful or 'writerly' to add to your biography. Just give a few facts about who you are and why you wrote this book. (Avoid clichés such as, 'my family love this', 'I think it will sell thousands' and 'you'd be a fool to pass this up'.)

If you've had an agent before, or have one now and are looking to change, a prospective agent needs to know this in your cover letter. Don't go into lengthy explanations; the agent just needs to know that you're being upfront, and have a sense of why you're searching for new representation.

An agent will also need to know if you're submitting your manuscript elsewhere. Be honest if you are. If you've targeted your agent carefully, it sounds confident and professional to say, 'I'm submitting *The Millkeeper* to two other agents.' This shows that you've done your research, and have thought about who your work might be right for.

Primarily, strive to keep your submission letter simple and direct, with a confident, pleasant tone. Spend time honing it and getting it as tight as possible. The worst cover letters I see are ones that go on for pages or are full of self-doubt, sell too hard or are too grovelling. One author wrote to me saying, 'this will be the only book I ever write'. An agent and editor will want to know that you have more than one book in you.

What catches my eye is strong writing, a punchy idea, a clear synopsis, and an unwaffly letter. Good credentials are important, such as the writer has studied at a recognized creative writing school or is an experienced journalist.

Veronique Baxter, David Higham Associates

No gimmicks or traps

Keep your submission professional, and don't try to be too clever in a bid to catch an agent's attention, as this often backfires. I know one agent who was sent a photograph of the author in her bikini! This is not likely to impress, however stunning the photograph. Another author sent a manuscript titled *The Moustache* and had a fake moustache enclosed in the covering page – and it wasn't supposed to be a joke. There's a difference between clever marketing and tacky novelty tricks.

If you are going to use marketing ploys, make sure your writing stands up to them. One agent was intrigued to receive a series of postcards over the course of a week 'from' different characters in an author's book. But the author hadn't distinguished between each character's voice, which only showed how unformed his writing was.

Try this

Have a go at writing a cover letter. Make sure it includes all of the following elements:

- correct contact details – yours and the agent (or publisher)
- introduce your book, genre and word length and give a brief story description
- introduce yourself – short paragraph biography
- say whether you're submitting to more than one agent
- mention that you hope the agent likes your work
- what you've enclosed – a synopsis, first three chapters and an SAE.

Polish it until it's as good as you can make it, and then show it to someone whose opinion you trust (for instance, your writing buddy) especially if they've read your book and can give feedback on how you've described it. Have you put yourself and your book forward in the best possible light?

The submission process can be a frustrating one, and you may be wondering at times if anyone is even reading your work. However, don't place traps in your manuscript to test this, such as a hair loosely stuck to a page or one page turned upside down, or a page in the wrong number order. These will just make you look paranoid; exactly the sort of client that agents don't want. (And, I know some agents who put these traps back in place even if they have read the material.)

Blurb

A blurb is the paragraph(s) that sells your book and entices a reader to pick it up and read on. While I wouldn't recommend that you send one in with your submission package, they can be a useful, personal reference piece – particularly if you're talking to an agent/editor about your book – as it trains you to think about your story in a colourful and sales-like way.

Look at the inside flap of a hardback or the back jacket of a paperback (and most books on Amazon have blurb paragraphs that you can refer to) for an idea of format and style. A blurb is hard to write and get right so make sure it sounds tight and sophisticated (no more than 100–200 words). Don't forget to end your blurb with a few unanswered questions: will the character solve the mystery; find her mother; beat the wizard?

Try this

Write a blurb as if you were having to sell your story to a bookshop, where you would need to get your message across in a succinct, imaginative and expedient way. Make it as punchy and colourful as possible.

Think of a sales rep with twenty seconds to pitch a book to someone who is serving customers at the same time, and doesn't want your book because they have no budget left and they are quite inclined to buy a few more Sharon Osbornes anyway. What is she going to say? If you can't do it, the rep can't.

Nick Sayers, Hodder

Synopsis

A well-written synopsis is a vital part of your submission package, as it can be the deciding factor in whether an agent or publisher will ask to see your entire manuscript. The key to writing a good synopsis is in knowing what it's meant to do. A synopsis is *not* meant to relate every event in your story, or to introduce every character. Rather, it's a brief overview of your story's main events, clearly showing the narrative arc and emotional journey of the main character(s).

Like your submission letter, keep things clear and direct: your synopsis isn't the place to show off your writing style. Also, don't try to entice agents to read your book with a cliffhanging question at the end of your synopsis. They need to know what your ending is, and that you've brought your different story threads together successfully.

Most agents require that synopses are no longer than a page (when I'm submitting on behalf of an author, I rarely submit a synopsis that is longer than two pages), and often it's the last thing that's looked at. If the opening chapters don't catch the agent's eye then they are unlikely to spend precious time looking at the synopsis.

I appreciate a brief, pleasant, informative, single-page letter, a concise CV, the first three chapters, and a succinct synopsis (which I read after the chapters not before, as a synopsis can give entirely the wrong impression).

Catherine Clarke, Felicity Bryan Literary Agency

A synopsis should be single-spaced, with breaks between paragraphs, and should be written in the present tense, in the third person. The first paragraph of your synopsis needs to address the basics: who your protagonist is, where they are, what situation/position they're in, their driving goal or problem, and the inciting event (the key thing that sparks off the story):

Ima Queen, the new bride of the King of Fairytaleland, seems to have it all: beauty, self-assurance, wealth. But her outer confidence hides a deadly insecurity. When her magic mirror reveals that Ima's stepdaughter Snow White has surpassed her in beauty, Ima is desperate to remain the most beautiful woman in the land.

You can then lay out the rest of the story in sequential order, focusing on the key story points as plotted on the three-act graph described in Chapter 04. These give you the skeleton of the narrative, on through to the final rug-pulling and resolution. If you're submitting to an agent who prefers a chapter by chapter breakdown (there aren't many of them, but they do exist), make sure that your synopsis, though longer, still feels smooth and tight (and you should double space if your synopsis is over a page long). Again, it can help to keep the three-act graph in mind here, just to give you a guide.

Try this

Write a one-page synopsis introducing the story and your main characters, with a clear beginning, middle and end, using the three-act graph from Chapter 04 to guide you. Make sure your margins are standard width – it's cheating to make them as wide as possible to squeeze more onto the page! Write at the top the heading 'synopsis', so the agent doesn't mistake it for your writing, along with your name, title, genre and word count.

When you've finished, show it to your writing buddy. What do they think? Does it give a good sense of the book's flavour and narrative arc, even though it probably doesn't include all the story threads?

Sample chapters

Having followed the guidelines in Part One of this guide, your sample chapters are sure to be tight and sparkling, with an arresting opening. Make sure that they now get the best possible chance with your chosen agent by taking care over their presentation.

Your sample chapters should always be **double-spaced**, printed in a standard font (Times New Roman or similar) and black ink. Have a header at the top that includes your title and surname (for instance, '*Millkeeper*/Corner'), and at the bottom have a footer with your page numbers. Your header should be right-justified so that it's easily visible when being read; your page numbers should be either centred or right-justified. Also, don't get clever with your header or footer. I read a manuscript once where the author had put 'Pre-publication draft' in his footer, which would be guaranteed to put an agent off.

Loose pages are much easier for an agent to read, so don't bind your manuscript in any way. Similarly, never attach the chapters together with paper clips, or put the chapters in individual plastic sleeves – this makes reading them very fiddly. Just pop a rubber band around the entire novel (or sample chapters, if that's all you're sending) and put it in a cardboard or plastic folder.

You should also have a **title page** at the start of your chapters. This should include your novel's title, in a large (but not too large) font in the centre of the page, with your name underneath it in a slightly smaller font. Again, use black ink. In the bottom left-hand corner, include 'copyright' or the symbol with your name, then the manuscript's word count, the month and year, and your contact details, along with your phone number and email. (Each piece of information should go on a separate line, like writing an address.)

It's easy to spot the difference between a really polished piece of work and one that's still in a rough draft, so before you submit you need to make your manuscript as perfect as possible. Edit, redraft, edit and redraft again until you're really happy with it.

> I tend to do a general read-through after a few weeks, not really stopping as I go, and then a second read through, making notes under different headings: themes, characters, plot, tension, page turning, imagery and so on. Then I will try to work out strategies for tackling the things I need to improve. And a final tip: I am a great fan of the Word 'comments function' – it's like putting little electronic Post-it® Notes on your manuscript as you go along. If I am not happy about a word or description, or want to check a fact, or anything I want to remember later, I put a little note on and then move on. The same function is great for using with critique partners.
>
> Kate Harrison

What catches an agent's eye

In summary, agents look for strong characterization and a properly thought-out plot, with a good balance between pace and reflection. They want to be absorbed by what they are reading and to be able to visualize the people, places and settings. Essentially, they want what any reader wants when reading a new book: to love what they're reading and be swept up by it. If the agent loves the style and the sound of your story then they'll read on.

> When I start reading, my first question is, can this author write? Does she/he have a distinctive style that holds the reader's attention? Then I ask myself, do I like the outline description of the book? Is there an idea in there that sounds interesting and compelling? It could be very fresh and different from what's being published at the moment or it could be in the same mould but feel exciting and new. My attention is definitely drawn to a cogent and well-presented letter telling me both about the author and the proposed project. And on first glance I do have a weakness for a flashy folder.
>
> Caroline Sheldon, Caroline Sheldon Literary Agency Ltd

You've sent off your manuscript – now what?

Agents are extremely busy and they have stacks of manuscripts – from both prospective and existing clients – to get through. Some agents only take on a handful of new clients a year, which means that they'll turn down 99.9% of new manuscripts. While they do look at the work in their submissions pile (there's still that 0.01% to think about), their first priority is to their existing clients; the ones who they need to make money for. They might be in the throes of an auction, selling foreign rights to dozens of countries, submitting to publishers, negotiating a contract, or attending a book fair.

How long do you wait? A month is about right before a polite follow-up. However, don't sound frustrated or indignant. The chances are that the receptionist, assistant to the agent, or the agent is looking at a metre-high pile of submissions. What will probably happen is that they'll dig out your submission and put it to the top of the pile. Ask how long it might take for them to give you an answer and don't be surprised if it's another few weeks or so.

> There is only one sure-fire way to avoid rejection – never send a
> manuscript out.
>
> Carole Matthews

What if they say no?

I know of very few published authors who haven't received a
rejection note in their time, so if your manuscript hasn't been
snapped up yet by an agent or publisher then you're in good
company. However, sometimes a rejection letter is saying more
than a straightforward turn down, and I would recommend that
you keep all your rejection letters on file and study them. Some
are standard answers and others are positive turn-downs, and
you need to know the difference.

A stock response from an agent could be: 'I'm afraid we're no
longer accepting unsolicited manuscripts due to the fact that our
client list is full. I do wish you luck in finding another agent.'

This can mean two things. Either the reader didn't feel sufficiently
interested in your opening pages, or it could quite simply mean
that their list is full. Don't get too discouraged by this; remember
that publishing is a hugely subjective business. What one agent
turns down, another might snap up with alacrity, so you should
definitely keep trying. However, if you receive a lot of this type of
rejection (up to eight, let's say), it probably means that your
manuscript has some significant problem areas, or hasn't been
targeted appropriately. If this is the case, do be honest with
yourself and question whether your work is ready to submit.

Agents sometimes cite the market as a reason for a turn-down:
'We loved reading your novel but unfortunately we don't feel
there is a market for it.' This might genuinely have something to
do with the market, but more often it means that the novel isn't
strong enough and therefore won't sell. Citing the market is a
stock answer so that the agent doesn't have to give specific
reasons as to why your novel has been turned down. It could be
well written and engaging but perhaps it's too mid-list – like a
cosy crime novel – that might not stand out enough. Or it might
be too literary with a proposed marginal readership, which
would be hard to sell to publishers. Perhaps your novel is too
specialist, or is a novella and too small, in which case you might
want to consider a specialist publisher – it could do well if
placed in a targeted market.

The upside to this is that the market does change. I often hear from agents that they're looking for a particular genre that only a year ago had 'no market'. If there is a gap publishers tend to buy ferociously, the market can then become swamped and publishers stop buying. Then there's another gap and the cycle begins again. If your story misses the market this year, in a couple of years it might be ready to receive your book, so hang on in there. It's good to have a feel for what people are buying and reading, but don't try to predict or second guess it – if we could do that we'd all be rich and there would be no publishing flops! Just keep writing what you love to write, make it the best it can be and be aware of general trends.

> After about my thirtieth rejection letter I decided not to send out any story I'd finished writing until I'd sat on it for at least a month and reworked it. I still got rejection letters after that but editors began to tell me why as opposed to just saying 'no'. When the quality of the rejection letters improved I knew my writing was getting better. In the end I found it easier to get a publisher than an agent. I was only taken on by an agent after my third book had been accepted for publication.
>
> Malorie Blackman

Many literary agencies have a scaling type of rejection, where they sort out submissions in piles of: 'no good', 'have promise but not there yet' and 'really good', where they request the entire manuscript. One of my workshop consultants used to work in a literary agency, and part of her job was to source the unsolicited pile, as the above. On the 'have promise' manuscripts, she would always write a personal letter or a note of encouragement on the rejection letter.

This middle type of response from agents or editors can often be overlooked or classed as unimportant by an author, but they are in fact a promising sign, and can also contain useful nuggets of information – such as 'Characterization felt flat, but good concept', or 'Fun idea, but needs to be structured more tightly'. If an agent mentions anything specific about your novel in their letter, this means it got far enough along in the process to be read at least in part by someone. You're on the right track. The agent may not have had the time to respond in detail, but they wouldn't encourage you unless they thought you had potential.

Treasure this feedback, and pick out pertinent points that have been made. If the letter says your story is slow to start, then look at your opening chapters and see where it might be tightened up. But only make revisions that you feel comfortable with. Sometimes an editorial suggestion hasn't been thought through carefully enough. They haven't read the whole manuscript, so it's hard to offer a well-rounded view, and their response might be rushed – so don't take it as prescriptive that once you've changed things accordingly it will make your manuscript publishable (see Chapter 09 for tips on taking editorial advice).

> While the suggestions of those who reject you may not be helpful, the fact that they've made them is. Chances are they're wrong about how you should fix the problem but right about the fact that there is a problem.
>
> Michael Marshall Smith

For manuscripts that make it into the 'really good' pile, the agent will contact the author and request the full manuscript, which may be passed on to a reader for a considered reading. If work is turned down at this stage, there is usually a recommendation that the author try another agent or a literary consultancy to get further editorial feedback, and if the agent has time, she will detail the reasons why it was rejected, along with giving the author encouragement. Frustrating though this sort of near miss can be, it can work in your favour: you have a contact now at an agency who knows and is interested in your writing, who you may be able to contact in the future with another novel. However, don't resubmit this novel to them unless they've specifically asked to see it again.

The best kind of rejection is when an editor or agent turns down your manuscript but asks to see further work. I would call them just to make contact and then start writing and revising to make sure that what you send them next is really going to wow them. A lot of agents and editors work in this way if a style of writing or a story caught their imagination.

If you are finding it impossible to get noticed, then you might need to accept that it may not happen *for the moment*. While I don't believe that talent can be taught, I do believe that if a writer has a spark of promise that it can be shaped. But this can take a long time, and it may be a question of taking a step back from the publishing arena and honing your craft more. Whatever you do, don't give up on your writing and don't let anyone tell you otherwise, because who knows where it could lead to?

What if my manuscript isn't ready?

You only have one crack at attracting an agent with your story, so it's a risk to send your work out if you've only perfected the first three chapters and have yet to write the novel. Being a first-time novelist you should really have the full manuscript to hand. If you think it's still a work-in-progress with more revision needed, contact the agent and explain. Chances are, they'll want it as near perfect as you can make it, which might mean that months will pass between their initial interest and your getting the manuscript to them – not an ideal situation.

Agent interest?

Dear Author,

I read with interest your submission of 'bodice-ripping romance' and I love the premise. I also think your writing has a spark to it and a pace and I would love to read the full manuscript. I should be able to give you an answer in about a month – would this be OK with you?

You mention that you've sent it to a couple of other agents. Have you heard anything from them? It would be great if we could have the option of first refusal.

All the best,

Hopeful agent

Brilliant news! But don't get out the champagne yet. You have to decide whether you give that proactive agent first refusal or whether you contact the other agencies where they all have a fair chance to request the full manuscript. It's down to gut feeling and a sense of doing the right thing. You could offer the agent first refusal but one month is too long. Ask if there's any chance of it being quicker – two weeks is fair. You could then sit back and wait to hear from the other agents.

Or, you could thank the first agent for looking at your manuscript, which you will be sending registered post today (or as soon as is possible), but as you've sent it out to two other agents it would be courteous to let them know that there is interest as you don't wish to waste anyone's time.

When you let the other agencies know there is interest in your manuscript be prepared for two reactions. It will either spur them on to look at your submission and request the manuscript (or not), or they might lose interest. This isn't as awful as it sounds. They may not want to spend time reading a manuscript when another agent is already interested, and they might suggest that you come back to them if the other agent turns it down. You shouldn't feel that this would work against you; it's perfectly acceptable for a great manuscript to be rejected. It's largely down to subjective appeal, and what might not suit one agent might suit another.

And then...

The moment you've been waiting for – a phone call from one of the agencies. They love your work, and wonder if you'd like to meet up to discuss it. Well done! This is hugely promising, but be aware that you still don't yet have an acceptance or an agent. It's important to prepare for this meeting and know what to expect, what kind of questions you should ask and areas that an agent should cover. Read on.

I go on gut instinct and personal taste so if I don't like the writing then I'm not going to be the book's best advocate. But if I think the book has merits I will always tell the author not to take my word for it and to try other agents. We have all probably turned down somebody else's triumphant best-seller.

Catherine Clarke, Felicity Bryan Literary Agency

getting an agent

In this chapter you will learn:
- what happens when you first meet an agent
- how to choose the best agent for you
- what to do if there's a problem with the agent/ author relationship.

> The best agents play a critical role – a good agent can do a lot of good and a bad one a lot of damage.
>
> Philippa Milnes-Smith, LAW Ltd

If an agent wants to meet you to talk about your work then this is an exciting position to be in. Finally, you're a step closer to having someone champion your work in the publishing arena. However, you're not there yet and it is still just a preliminary step. Treat it like an informal interview where they've yet to take you on and you've yet to decide whether they're the right agent for you.

> I like an exploratory conversation with prospective clients so we are both at our ease and can get a sense of how it might be to work together, as you are in it for the long haul ideally – it's potentially a marriage, not just a date. I anticipate being asked practical things like how the submission process works and how we handle American and translation deals, and I usually explain how our commission structure works. The main thing is to come away with a sense of mutual trust and excitement.
>
> Catherine Clarke, Felicity Bryan Literary Agency

First meeting

Most meetings go well and it's insightful to discuss your work and to see where it can go. It's also useful to get an insider's view of the market and how a book is published. However, until you both agree that you're happy to go ahead and you have a contract to sign, this is just an exploratory stage.

Sometimes agents will go to this stage but keep the offer of representation open. They may want to see a revised manuscript and then make their decision. Some agents might turn an author down during this meeting: perhaps there isn't a rapport or the author's resisting further changes. I know one agent who, meeting with an author for the first time, had the contract under the table and they settled in to talk about his manuscript, which she loved. However, there were a few minor changes to be made. He was vehemently resistant to each one. She left the contract unsigned under the table and bade him well. This relationship would have been fraught with problems and tensions for both parties.

An agent may say there and then if they want to represent you. If this happens and you're unsure or you're meeting other agents, thank them for their time – the agent's read your work, made suggestions for revision, spent time to meet you and has so far not made a penny – and ask if you can let them know, perhaps in a week's time. If you're considering other agents, don't forget to warn this agent *before you meet* that this is the case. Meeting other agents before you make your choice is often referred to as a beauty parade, where agents feel they're being interviewed and have to impress you and perhaps waste precious time if you don't sign up with them.

However, I don't really understand this approach. Just as they have the right to choose a client, you also have the right to pick the right agent for you. They should know (and accept) that you're meeting other agents, but be careful not to come across as arrogant and choosy.

> You have to get on with an agent very well, so the first meeting is crucial. Do not sign up with an agent unless you're confident they are going to be your number one fan and supporter.
>
> Adele Geras

If you suspect the agent isn't right for you – perhaps his vision for your manuscript is different to yours or they're not sounding passionate enough about what you've written – they may not be the best person to champion your writing to publishers. However, if you're just concerned because you don't seem to be clicking with them, hold back on your decision. You may not be chatting away like old friends, but they might be dazzling in a negotiation situation. You're really looking for someone who's professional, with whom you could have a good working relationship, and who will look after your interests.

There are basic areas to cover (see next page) that will help you know whether someone is the right agent for you. Make sure you address these issues during your meeting, as the agent's responses will give you a good idea of how they work.

You and your book

This is a chance for the agent to tell you what they love about your writing and why your story is so good! However, they might also suggest that you revise your manuscript further.

I know one agent who's been working with an author for over a year and has read his manuscript at least three times. She knows he has talent and likes him, which is why she's put so much energy into his writing. However, she still hasn't taken him on. It would be unfair to represent him before he could deliver a book she felt she could submit and place. Goodwill from his part will probably mean that he offers any revised or new manuscript to this agent for first refusal, but officially he's still free to pursue other agents.

Whenever I speak to agents I hear time and again how they have a few authors who they strongly believe in but cannot place with a publisher. This is frustrating for them but they continue to keep these authors, even though it doesn't make monetary sense, because they believe in the writer's talent. This is why you need an agent who strongly believes in your work: otherwise they might give up on you before you find your saleable story.

You might find that in your first meeting an agent is interested in your writing potential, but doesn't feel that the book you've written is strong enough to launch you. It's especially important for a debut novelist that their first book is really stunning so it's possible that they suggest you write a new novel. They'll be cautious about sending out a manuscript that doesn't reflect what you could be capable of. It might not attract any publishers, or if it's commissioned and dies a death due to poor sales, the publisher might not commission your next book. An agent will have a good feel for what's right for the market, so if they suggest you write something new, don't dismiss it out of hand. You'll need to decide whether you go with this agent and follow their advice, or if you want to persist with your novel and find another agent.

Agents vary tremendously. I do know authors who are almost scared of their agents, and hardly speak to them from one month to the next, whereas I have a much more personal and friendly relationship with mine, which I prefer. Some agents don't take a lot of interest in the writing; others do, and read and comment on everything you write. It's important to know what you want from your agent before you sign on. Also, find out whether a prospective agent is a specialist in your field, e.g. children's books, or science fiction. If not, he or she won't have the right kind of contacts.

Linda Newbery

The agent's role

An agent will talk through the various stages of preparing your manuscript for submission, and will explain how they sell rights and how the commission rate works. They'll also coach you on what a publisher will expect from you and what the editor's role will be. An agent essentially looks after your needs as a writer, and an editor will look after your manuscript's needs.

Earnings, commission percentage, and subsidiary rights

The standard UK agent's commission rate is between 10–15%. Foreign rights that have been retained by the agent are usually charged out at 20% because of the extra costs involved, such as a sub-agent's fee. Each agent varies in what they can offer, so they should give you a good idea of what they intend to do for you and your book. For instance, they might decide to retain some rights and offer a publisher other rights, or retain all rights, or offer the publisher all the rights – depending on who has the better contacts and who can optimize the book's potential.

You should ask about film and TV rights, but be aware that your book might not be suitable for this medium or a deal might come at a later stage. Any agent will tell you that there is no strict formula, and it's usually down to the 'x' factor that will catch a producer's eye. But generally, to have your book optioned your story must be visual and translate well into a film. It should have a strong story arc – beginning, middle and end – that fits into a one- to two-hour storyline. It should have strong characters with good dialogue potential, so the emotional plotline is important. Some agencies have a film division (so a film agent would represent your book) and other agents handle both book and film rights. Both will have established contacts with film scouts and producers, but do ask what they've placed in the past. If your book is optioned the fee can vary, from one with very few noughts to one with a string of them, depending on how powerful and enthusiastic the buying party is. The time span to turn it into a film can last for one and a half to three years (which can then be renegotiated). Many books that are optioned never make it to production stage – odds of about one in nine are quoted. If your book gets to this stage it will be turned into a script that you may not be involved with or have any control over.

Who the agent intends to submit to

The main role of an agent is to get the best deal for you in monetary terms, which generally means your book goes to the publisher who offers the highest advance. However the best deal is not always the most obvious. An agent might advise you to opt for a publisher who offers less but intends to have a higher marketing spend (budget) under an imprint that perfectly suits the book. Or you might get on better with an editor who really understands your book than with another editor who is offering more.

An agent may have a list of publishers to whom they think your book would appeal. Or they may decide to pitch exclusively to one publisher who they think would be a perfect fit commercially and editorially. If this isn't discussed in the initial meeting, the agent should give you a clear idea of where they intend to pitch your book soon after the meeting and preferably before the contract is signed.

Your agent might be so confident of your novel's blockbuster potential that they decide to run an auction. Agents are wary of auctions as it can be embarrassing if no publisher joins in or a lower than predicted offer comes in – one that might be lower than if the agent had submitted exclusively or with less fanfare. However, if an auction is run well it can be exhilarating.

Publishers have a fixed time and date to put in their offer and they don't know who they're bidding against. If the idea is hot and the agent has set it up well it can bring in a high offer and create an industry buzz. The publisher who offers the highest all-round deal is the one who gets the book. Here is not the time to backtrack and say that you prefer another publisher who offered less.

How you can build on your writing career

The agent will want to know that you have other books in you. Depending on your genre, they'll also have an idea of how many novels they expect you to write. For instance, if you've written a saga then you might need to write one a year. If you've written the first of a sci-fi trilogy then you will definitely have to deliver books two and three with a time frame in mind.

If you've written a social realism teen novel or a thriller or an intelligent chick-lit then you should be prepared to stay in this genre for a while. A publisher will most likely want to publish a second novel (if the first sold well) and one-off wonders can be wasted energy and marketing spend. What happens, though, if you want to also write for a lower age group or if you want to at some point change genre or write for both the adult and children's market? An agent will advise you on what to do. Perhaps you could have two writing names, or if you're successful in the genre you're known for you could afford to switch or write simultaneously for two markets. Helen Dunmore and Isabel Allende write both for the adult and children's market. And there are those authors who assume a nom-de-plume when they write for different genres such as Michael Marshall Smith/Michael Marshall and Ruth Rendell/Barbara Vine.

An agent might also suggest you build on your writing portfolio. You could write short stories and enter competitions, or if you've written picture books the agent might suggest you also write for a higher age group. Once you've got a publishing deal you may want to write articles for writing magazines or newspapers with your story of how you got published. This will advertise your book and build on your name as a writer (see Chapter 13 for more information on publicity and development angles).

If you come away from your first meeting feeling positive about your future potential working relationship, then you're of course on the right track. If you're feeling neutral or unenthusiastic about it, think hard before agreeing to be signed up by that agent.

I think instinct is very important. You need to choose what's good for you. I was a little scared of my agent when I first met her, and I'm not easily scared, so I thought that was a good thing. She seemed fiercely intelligent and didn't suffer fools, and I desperately wanted to impress her. I also figured editors would have a similar reaction to her, though she was very new to agenting. And it's turned out to be true.

Meg Rosoff

What if the agent doesn't want to meet?

I find it strange when an agent takes on a client without meeting them, unless an author would find it hard to make the trip (perhaps they're based in another country). I know some leading agents who don't always meet their clients before taking them on, but if I was an author about to sign up, I'd want to meet for at least a coffee and preferably in their office to get a feel for their working environment, and how you get on with them face to face. However, if you do choose to go with an agent without meeting them, discuss the points in this chapter over the phone, and be sure you're happy with what is said.

Which agent should you choose?

If more than one agent wants to take you on, this is a fantastic position to be in. You should meet them all – preferably within a few days – and make up your mind as to who is most perfect for you and your book. So long as they all know that you are considering other agents then no one should feel misled. Whoever you decide to go with, contact them first.

Don't judge on size: small agencies can be just as effective as larger ones. A large agency is likely to have a number of agents handling books, films, media and foreign rights. They're also likely to have a larger client list. A one-man band will handle personally all aspects of selling your book and will have fewer clients but just as good contacts.

I know editorial directors who have worked for top publishers who then set up on their own or join an agency. This can be a great position to be in because they will be building their list and fresh to the cause, with insider publisher knowledge and strong contacts. What an exciting balance: you as a new author and your agent who is setting out to prove himself. His approach may be fresher than a long-standing agent whose list is heaving.

There are also well known one-man bands who perhaps only take on a couple of authors a year. They will have a firm hold of their list, usually a formidable reputation and all with a personal touch. At this stage, it's down to personal preference – which agent and agency environment do you click with most?

Beware of agents who ask for a fee

I often receive calls from authors who have agent interest but are being asked to pay money, perhaps for an initial read of their manuscript. The majority of agents adhere to a recognized code of practice, especially if they are a member of the Association of

Authors' Agents (AAA), and one of the guidelines is that agents should not charge a fee. You can identify members in the *Writers' and Artists' Yearbook* by the asterisk* against their name. You can also contact the AAA or look up www.agentsassoc.co.uk on the Internet if you want to check those who are members and the requirements.

Just because an author isn't an AAA member, it doesn't mean they're not legitimate. Perhaps they've just set up and haven't been practising for the required three years or have a revenue of under £25,000. Charging a fee is not against the law, it's an AAA guideline – in essence, an agent should be making money *for* you.

However, there is a distinction between charging an author a fee (be wary) and asking an author to cover costs such as photocopying and postage, especially when it comes to sending out a manuscript. These are standard costs that all agents charge, though most agents will simply deduct this amount from your first advance cheque rather than charging you up front. When you receive your first royalty statement these fees should be clearly laid out, and you should question anything that looks over the odds.

You've got your agent contract

This is the formality that seals the relationship with your agent. Most contracts are very straightforward, but do check with the agent if you don't understand anything. Now it's a question of delivering your manuscript and letting the agent take over.

Submitting to publishers

Your manuscript is ready to send out to publishers. The agent calls each editor, sells you in, and creates a hype about your book. A pristine copy of your manuscript is sent off, or possibly emailed, and the agent usually asks the publisher to get back to them within a certain date (a month is usually the longest). I say 'pristine copy' because a manuscript that looks like it's been read and turned down by others is not a good sign, and editors spot this. It's then a question of waiting. This time your agent will also be biting his nails! Even if your agent receives a rejection or interest you might not hear about it immediately, depending on how they operate. Either way, your agent will advise you with a level of communication that's practical to his time and where you're not left in the dark.

> An author should be committed and consistent in working really hard at their writing. Any writer who has built a long-term career knows it's about so much more than that exciting moment when you get your first book placed. To compete in what is a very tough market the first book is just the first step.
>
> Philippa Milnes-Smith, LAW Ltd

It's worth mentioning the obvious here. Just because you have an agent it doesn't mean that they'll be able to place your novel with a publisher. However, your chances are now greatly increased. They'll be targeting editors they know, and your manuscript will be going through the solicited system as opposed to the unsolicited system, which is processed by different people.

Unhappy with your agent?

Perhaps you feel that your agent is unapproachable, or that he isn't doing enough to sell your book. If you have concerns with your agent I would always favour the soft approach first, even if you're privately climbing the walls with frustration. Call your agent or meet with them and first check that you are doing everything you can to build your writing career and to help your agent sell your work. Perhaps you're an exhausting client, ringing all the time asking for feedback on the tiniest of things? Then you need to take this on board and redress the way *you* work with your agent. But you must feel that he has your best interests at heart and that you trust what is being done for you. After all, he effectively works for you, by the very nature that he takes a commission of anything sold.

If you feel reassured but are still wondering why there doesn't seem to be any progress, it may be that there is simply nothing to report back to you. Your agent should have excellent contacts and aggressively sell you in whenever there is an opportunity, but perhaps the trade isn't biting (at the moment). Give your agent a chance to discuss ways forward and listen to his side of things. If you feel reassured and, better still, fired up with the outcome then you have saved your author–agent relationship and the agent need never know that you were dissatisfied.

Remember:

- Your agent wouldn't have taken you on if he didn't believe in what you wrote.
- Your agent doesn't get paid until he sells your work so it is in his interest to work hard to sell your book and to advise you well.
- He wants the relationship to work, and for you to be happy with the arrangement.

However, not all agents are top class. Having an agent who doesn't seem to be working for you, where you suspect that they don't have the right contacts or aren't respected in the industry, can be damaging. How do you know if they're effective or not? You should have a fair idea from the outset of whom they represent, and what sort of publisher contacts they have by what novels they've sold. You should also have a good idea of the way they operate and communicate from how they deal with you.

If they never return your calls, are generally haphazard in the way they work and you're constantly dissatisfied, then it's time to move on. After all, if they're like that with you what are they like with publishers?

Should you change your agent?

Leaving your agent is a risk, in that you may not find another agent, or a new agent might not be able to resubmit your work to publishers who have already seen it via your first agent, particularly if it was a straight turn down. But you need to feel happy and trust your agent to do well by you, so it's better to not have one at all than to have one who is holding back your career.

There are two schools of thought about changing an agent, both of which have their place. Some agents are open to talking confidentially to new clients as they feel that the author has a right to check their status (although they wouldn't expect you to say who currently represents you). However, on hearing an author's concerns – where perhaps the agent hasn't managed to sell their book – they might advise them that it's unlikely they would be able to do things differently. In doing this they may have actually saved the existing relationship, and if the agent is well known then a new agent would find it hard to do better.

If they feel that the agent isn't exhausting all the right avenues or the author's grievances are justified, then they can advise accordingly, but should never take on a new client until the author has gone through the official steps of terminating their relationship with their old agent.

Other agents feel very strongly about being contacted while an author is still with their existing agent and would expect you to 'sack' your agent first before looking for new representation.

If you're anxious to know who you might contact without running the risk of offending anyone then it would be a good idea to get independent advice. You could ask the Society of Authors (SOA), or a literary consultant. For instance, in my line of work – even though I cannot influence an author's decision when it comes to dealing with the trade, as I have to remain impartial – I can still guide an author on what is generally accepted in the publishing world, and of course, everything remains confidential.

If you both agree to part company, get it in writing. Now you can officially approach other agents. Know that your previous agent has the right to retain commission due on rights sold by them on your previous book(s), and will continue to handle the royalties for these titles.

Changing your agent can be a positive move

A new agent might be more innovative in the way they submit your work, or they might have different ideas about what you've written and where your writing career should go, or their publisher contacts may be different to your previous agent's. Or, it may be just a case of new-found enthusiasm.

I found my first agent through the *Writers' and Artists' Yearbook*. She kept telling me to write another while she submitted to one publisher at a time. Each would hang on to it for three months. Then I tried it on my own which was hopeless. After that I was taken on by a *big* agent who dropped me after a year of near misses. Then someone who worked for Hodder put me in touch with my agent who suggested I changed my name for a fresh start. I then had four publishers wrangling over it. They asked me to keep my pseudonym as it sounded brighter than my real name.

Jane Bidder

The good news is, the majority of agents are great and you won't need to make that change!

13

the reality of being published

In this chapter you will learn:
- how the publishing process works
- how an editor buys a book
- about the different stages your book goes through once it's been commissioned.

> My agent is my guardian angel. She looks after me and my
> interests. My editor is the book's guardian angel. She looks after
> the book, and the interests of the publishing house – and then me.
>
> Katherine Langrish

An inside view of a publishing house

Each publishing house has a different structure, but generally an imprint will have a publishing director, perhaps associate publishers, editorial directors, editors, assistant editors and editorial assistants/secretaries, and most of their time will be spent on seeing books through the publishing process.

The other part of the editorial business is commissioning new books, and solicited manuscripts come in daily via agents. Editors read their assigned manuscripts and either turn them down or take ones that appeal on to a second reading. As editors rarely have a dedicated reader (unlike publishers) a second opinion usually comes from an assistant who is keen to make a mark and shadow the editor.

Manuscripts that get a positive reading will be passed by the in-house reader on to the publisher, who may already have an idea as to whether it's one she will take to the next stage. She will read it and perhaps get another opinion, and if it's an all-round positive she will present it at the weekly editorial meeting.

The editorial meeting

This is the forum for publishers and editors to champion the manuscripts they're interested in buying. Those also present will usually be the sales director, finance director, and people from publicity and marketing as it's vital to get their input before making an offer on a book. After the meeting, copies of the manuscripts are distributed to each department. These are read, and feedback usually takes a few days to a week. If sales can't see a market for it or publicity don't feel passionate enough about it then it may get turned down at this stage. Getting an editor behind your book is one thing, but getting twelve or so people from all divisions of the publishing arena to agree can be really hard. The more powerful an editor is within the house, the more likely she is to get the full team behind a book.

Up until now you may be blissfully unaware that your book is going through this process. However, as soon as it's given the go-ahead the editor will need to estimate some costings in time for the acquisitions meeting, which is where the proposed offer will be reviewed and agreed. The acquisitions meeting gives everyone concerned an idea of what's being bought, for how much, and how it fits in with the overall publishing programme.

The editor will then contact the agent (or you if you're unagented) with the good news.

You've got an offer!

This is the time to get out the champagne and celebrate. The hard graft is over; you can finally see an end in sight and your book on the shelves. You would be right to think that it's been a long haul, and question why everything takes so long in the publishing world. It just does: from writing, to redrafting, to submitting, to getting an agent and then a publisher, and now … you will have to wait about a year before you see your book in the bookshops. But the emotional rewards can be amazing and the financial rewards, although usually modest, can be life-changing if your book becomes a blockbuster, so hang in there.

Ordinarily, a publisher(s) will make an offer, and you will choose a publisher and the contract will be agreed. Your editor will arrange a meeting, either before the contract is signed or after. She will go through what she proposes for your book – for instance, perhaps there's further editorial revision to be done (I can hear you groan but this happens a fair bit) – and the various stages it will go through before it's published. This is the time to talk about what is expected from you and when you should deliver, and often your agent will be present to help you understand this. On signing the contract, you will receive a part of your advance. Then it's a question of delivering your manuscript on time.

The author should think beyond the excitement of being published and try to practically find out what exactly the publisher is going to do with their book. In the world of books and publishing, as in life, it is unrealized expectations that are the killer.

David Fickling, David Fickling Books

Meet and woo the author

When a publisher thinks they may have to fight off competition, usually in an auction, they can be really creative and may woo you (and your agent) from afar. HarperCollins famously cordoned off the entrance of their offices to re-enact a crime scene. It had blue flashing lights, police tape and a dossier of 'witness' reports to the book for a crime novel they wanted to buy. They also sent to another author a hamper containing items that appeared in the book – sloe gin, bramble jam, a Georgette Heyer book and a teddy bear – as well as a first edition of a Nancy Mitford novel, a quote from which was used in the prelims to the novel.

While this sort of attention can naturally be heady, you'll need to discuss the different offers with your agent with more in mind than just who gave the flashiest presentation. Factors such as which editorial team you felt really clicked with your book, and what sort of marketing plan they might have in mind can be vital to the success of your future career, and must be taken into account when making your decision.

> I submitted a German novel *The Chess Machine* by Robert Loehr to eight publishers in an auction. Six made offers and some in most inventive ways. Fig Tree put in an offer and the publisher told me it would 'knock my socks off'. After hearing her offer I told her that only one sock had been knocked off! When the deal was sealed and we met, I was presented with a lovely pair of socks which I am keeping as a lucky charm for my next auction.
>
> Tanja Howarth, Tanja Howarth Literary Agency

Negotiating the deal

Once you've opted for a publisher it's then a question of working out the deal. This is the best bit. Your agent will look through the offer and negotiate what needs to be changed and added in. A higher royalty rate may be argued for, or an escalating royalty rate (or a further advance) if your manuscript sells over a certain number of copies, or a higher percentage on certain rights such as high discount sales to supermarkets.

More importantly, a publisher will negotiate which subsidiary rights they may want to acquire. Usually, if an agent has good contacts they will want to retain as many rights as possible, or if they feel that the publisher has stronger contacts in particular areas they will sell them.

If the publisher is unyielding in areas such as net receipts (what the publisher actually receives), as opposed to royalties based on recommended retail price then your agent might withdraw and submit to another publisher. This is called a deal breaker and depends on how much confidence your agent has in placing your book elsewhere.

If you don't have an agent, you can contact the Society of Authors, who have a team of contract advisers who offer free advice to members. Even though the SOA is happy to offer broad advice to writers, you can only become a member if you have a publishing contract. Or you can contact The Writers' Guild – mainly for Screenwriters, but also for all types of writing for the media, including books.

Publishing contracts

A contract is a mutual commitment between author and publisher where both parties promise to deliver what was originally negotiated and agreed. For instance, if your opening chapters or full manuscript was intended to be a 80,000-word historical novel, then this is what you must deliver. (You mustn't have a change of heart and deliver a modern romance thriller that has a weaker storyline and characters and runs to 120,000 words.) In return they will publish your book accordingly – within a year to 18 months of receipt of manuscript – and pay the agreed royalty rates and revenue from subsidiary rights.

If you deliver a manuscript that is unacceptable (one that is beyond editorial change) or is 30 days beyond the agreed delivery time, the publisher has the right to terminate the contract and generally to request all monies to be repaid. This is very unusual though. It's unlikely you'd deliver something radically different in terms of story or quality, and if you're running behind schedule and it's for legitimate reasons, the publisher will most likely be understanding and try to move the publishing schedule. This would require a possible loss of revenue, not to mention a gap in their list in that month, so don't treat it lightly.

To give you an idea of what to expect from a contract I've based the following general guidelines on the Minimum Terms Agreement (MTA) drawn up by the Society of Authors and The Writers' Guild of Great Britain, and have at times made particular reference to the Hodder & Stoughton contract. The MTA outlines a publisher's basic code of conduct when offering a contract; not all publishers are signed up but the main ones tend to be. If you would like to know more about contracts, Carole Blake's *From Pitch to Publication* (Macmillan) and Michael Legat's book, *An Author's Guide to Publishing* (Hale) are useful reference books. As each contract varies, use this only as a general guide.

Format:

Hardcover: publication date, an approximate UK retail price and estimated first print run.

Paperback: as above.

Rights, territories and duration:

You retain full copyright and the publisher buys the licence to publish your book. The publisher may acquire exclusive world English-language volume rights and any other subsidiary rights (open to negotiation).

This right to publish can last up to 70 years beyond the author's demise, after which the work enters the public domain.

Advance:

This is like a deposit payment, set against projected future earnings, and is generally broken down into three or four stages: signature of contract, delivery of manuscript, hardback publication (or within one year of signature) and paperback publication.

Before you can earn royalties you have to earn out your advance. Your book has to sell enough copies or subsidiary rights for the publisher to recoup its costs.

Royalties:

Home sales of **hardcover** in the British Isles (Great Britain, Northern Ireland, Channel Islands, the Isle of Man, the Isles of Scilly and the Irish Republic) based on the UK retail price:

- 10% on the first 2,500 copies sold
- 12½% on the next 2,500 copies sold
- 15% on all further copies sold.

Export sales of **hardcover** outside the British Isles based on net receipts (what the publisher receives after fees or discounts given to agents, wholesalers or booksellers):

- 10% on the first 2,500 copies sold
- 12$\frac{1}{2}$% on the next 2,500 copies sold
- 15% on all further copies.

Home sales of **mass-market paperback** based on the UK retail price:

- 7$\frac{1}{2}$% on the first 40,000 copies sold
- 10% on all further copies sold.

Export sales of **mass-market paperback**:

- 10% based on net receipts.

Home sales of **trade paperback** based on the UK retail price:

- 7$\frac{1}{2}$% on the first 10,000 copies sold
- 10% on all further copies sold.

Export sales of **trade paperback**:

- 10% based on net receipts.

Royalties based on net receipts in home and export sales on **high discount deals**:

- Depending on who the publisher sells to at discount (50% or more), or if the size of a print run is less than 1,500, this may mean a lesser percentage is paid out in terms of royalties (perhaps four-fifths of the prevailing rate).
- For low reprints, omnibus editions or promotional reprints, royalty rates may vary.

It's worth mentioning here, that for agents this is one of the most highly argued over sections in the contract. With supermarkets entering the field, discounts can soar to 60% and above. Both publisher and author share the pain. The agent's job is to deflect as much of this pain as possible off the author. Supermarkets maintain that to counteract this, they sell a high number of books to an audience who might buy on impulse, so they argue that it can work in an author's favour.

Electronic rights:

This is a hot-bed of change and is in perpetual discussion. The grey area lies in the international nature of the Internet and the fact that opportunities to exploit electronic rights are constantly evolving. For instance, the e-book (book in digital form) after a lot of false starts and speculation is about to finally take off due to technological improvements. So, it's advisable to keep on top of these opportunities and for both parties to leave this as unspecified as possible and up for review. The publisher has the right to sell an electronic edition within 24 months after the first UK publication. After that you can request the rights to be reverted 90 days from receipt of notice. NB: In regard to publishing on the Internet, if you have two publishers (UK and US) then they both must come to some mutual agreement.

For **electronic work** on **publishers'** versions:

- 50% of the publisher's net receipts.

For **electronic work** on **licensed** versions:

- 50% of the publisher's royalty receipts.

Electronic form:

- E-book and other – 80%.

Subsidiary rights:

Unless it's negotiated otherwise, such as a percentage based on net receipts, you will receive a percentage of the advance and royalties of any rights the publisher sells. The main ones are:

- serial (an extract of your work published in a newspaper or magazine)
- US and translation rights
- TV, film and radio (although it's more usual for an agent to keep all dramatic rights).

US and translation rights:

- translation rights – 80% (for instance, a publisher will receive 20% of the deal and the author will receive 80%, 10% of that will go to the agent)
- publication rights in US – 80–85%.

These sales can also bring a second tier of revenue. If, say, a French publisher is granted volume and world rights it may go on to sell to other countries that are French speaking, with subsidiary rights such as paperback and serialization deals. Remember, these will be counted against your original advance, so you won't start to earn these sums until it's paid back.

Your **agent** may decide to retain the rights and **sell direct**:

- US and translation rights – generally you will receive 80% and your agent 20% (the higher percentage commission is to cover costs of dealing overseas and often sub-agent costs).

First refusal on your second book:

If your publisher commissioned your first book only, as opposed to making a two-book deal from the outset, they might ask to be given first refusal on your second novel. If they don't take it on you will be free to offer it to another publisher. Or, you might decide to stay with your publisher and write a third novel. At this stage, there will be a new contract subject to negotiation. If you are unagented, you might want to check with the SOA as to what would be a fair deal.

My first book was accepted immediately, but my third was rejected by the firm which had bought the first two. Undeterred I returned to the library and spent several hours browsing, discovered another publisher who was putting out the sort of book I had written, and got it accepted first go. It was, as it turned out, the best thing that could possibly have happened to me. There I was, the complete beginner, agentless, didn't know anyone in publishing, and I suddenly had two publishers, both of whom wanted my work, and both of whom paid me rather more because they both wanted my original name!

Katie Flynn

You and your editor

Once you've signed the contract your book is effectively handed over to the publisher, and from here on, you will liaise with your editor.

Once you've delivered your manuscript there may two responses: one is that it still needs revising, in which case it's a question of being patient and working out whether you can do what is necessary to bring it up to publication standard. Or, your editor approves it. Brilliant! Your manuscript now enters the publishing wheel that can take about a year to complete.

During this cycle, your editor will liaise with you on issues such as checking the copy-editing comments and the final stages of proofing. If you have an agent, he will be kept in the loop and may intervene if there's anything you are unhappy with, thereby protecting the author/editor relationship, but otherwise it will be down to you and your editor.

An author should expect regular contact from an editor – not just when editing is in progress or publication approaches. They should be someone they can speak to openly about any worries they have, or anything that isn't clear.

Maxine Hitchcock, HarperCollins

The editing and marketing preparation stage

There are two types of editing – structural and copy-editing. Sometimes your editor will fulfil both roles or you will have two separate editors. The first is structural, where your editor will read through your manuscript and either make further revision suggestions (at the beginning stage) or, give it one last check (the final stage). She may flag up a scene that needs to be tightened or a character to be more developed; or it may just be cosmetic changes such as tightening up a sentence or two. The copy-editing and line-by-line edit can either occur at this stage or come later.

Editors are like teachers, and can show you what to do to improve your work. The best advice I ever had was from my editor who recommended that the Gods became actual characters in my novel *Troy*, which helped the book, and me immensely. Copy-editors are worth their weight in gold when it comes to pointing out tics in one's writing. I, for instance, have to be careful not to use the words 'just' and 'all' too much!

Adele Geras

Your editor will also be keeping a firm eye on the pre-publication stages that your book needs to go through. The most important aspect to get underway is the jacket cover. She will brief the design department either as an open brief or with a specific idea. A mock-up will be made by a freelance designer or done in-house which will usually be sent to you for comment. A publisher will have a good idea as to what will make your book sell so unless you have strong feelings about the design it will save time and money to go with what they have in mind. But nothing is set in stone, so you can go back with any comments. You may have something to add or take out of the blurb – the sell-in summary that your editor or the blurb department will have written – which is easier to change, so don't be afraid to make suggestions.

If there is a significant marketing spend for your book, your editor will also be liaising with marketing, publicity and sales. This will be for point-of-sale material for booksellers, proposed advertising campaigns, author tours, and preparation for things like the sales conference and entry for the publisher's catalogue. This is why it's so important to get the jacket cover done as soon as possible as this will be used for all the above. Your publisher may even set up a website for you. Katherine Langrish had this happen for her debut novel, *Troll Fell* (HarperCollins). As it's a children's book the interactive site hugely appealed to her young, technically savvy audience.

Your editor will prepare an advance information sheet (AI) which is like a show card to present to the trade so they can get a factual teaser of your book. It will have a sell-in blurb, and details such as format, when it's due to be published, any point-of-sale available such as posters or dumpbins, and any author publicity planned. This will be used as a reference piece in-house and sent out mainly to booksellers.

The next stage is to copy-edit the manuscript, where spelling and syntax (sentence construction and rhythm of your writing) are checked. A copy-editor will also draw up a graph of your characters and story and cross-check facts. For instance, if a character's hair suddenly changes colour, or if you've written an historical novel and the French windows have double-glazing, all these inconsistencies will be marked up for your attention.

Your marked-up manuscript will be returned to you, either through the post or by email, with additional notes from the copy-editor. It's then up to you to revise accordingly or disregard. Apart from inconsistencies, any comments at this stage tend to be suggestions only, and a lot of respect is given to your vision of the book. The publisher should send back the revised, copy-edited manuscript back to you for approval and one last check.

You will then be sent a proof copy of the typeset manuscript, and you'll need to check for any typographical errors that might have crept in. This is not the time for any further editorial revisions (although if you really feel strongly about something, change it). Anything you wish to revise in excess of 10–15% of the typesetting cost you will be expected to pay. Once this has been sent back to the publisher it will then be proofread in-house or by a freelancer.

Around this time, your publisher may send out uncorrected bound proofs to reviewers and shown to sub-agents for foreign rights sales.

Publicize your book

Generally, a publisher will only assign a publicity budget to lead titles. So be prepared, even with your blockbuster-in-the-making, to do much of your own publicity. Whatever you manage to arrange, let your editor and the publicity department know in case anything needs to be co-ordinated, such as sending out a copy of your book to be reviewed, or books to be sent to a venue if you're doing a talk. In any case, it's always a good idea to talk to publicity where they should at least be able to give you some advice on how you go about things.

Contact your local or regional radio station and newspaper to see if they would like to review your book, or interview you. The local media love success stories, especially from struggling authors who have gone on to get published.

If you're a children's writer you'll most likely want to do school visits, where you go in and speak to children about writing. The good news is that not only are you paid to do this by the school but you also get to reach your target audience and get feedback on your book. It's hard work, but rewarding. Jacqueline Wilson works tirelessly in this way regardless of the fact that she's constantly in the best-seller lists.

Go to all the bookshops (and shops) in your area with a promotional postcard and ask if they will display it.

You should also go into your local bookshop and offer to do a book signing (I say local bookshop, as you generally need to be an established author to do any kind of tour). It needs to be well organized, so ask the bookshop how you should go about it. For instance, much of the success of a signing comes down to how well the bookshop advertises it: displaying a poster a week before it takes place is likely to have more effect than displaying a poster at the last minute. The publisher will need to send copies of your book in advance; you can liaise with the publicity department for this, or have the bookstore do it. Get a few friends or family to join you while you're there, as signings can be daunting – especially if very few people approach you, which is common in book signings so be prepared for this!

Contact every society or organization that you're linked to and ask if they would send out an announcement email or display your card. For instance, if you've written a romance adventure that is set in a ski-resort, and you are a member of The Ski-Club of Great Britain, then there might be an opportunity to promote your book to their members.

Offer to do author talks, perhaps at a local writing festival or at your old school, or university.

Book launches tend not to happen these days as they are costly and don't necessarily add to the revenue of your book. If you do have one, you may have to foot the bill or at least half of it. You may be lucky enough to get a few book reviewers or booksellers present but don't expect a high turnout as these people are inundated with invitations of this kind. If your publisher is footing the bill you may also be quite limited as to how many friends and family you are allowed to invite, so accept this graciously; remember, the main purpose of the event from their point of view is to gain media attention.

Launches can, however, be great fun and an opportunity to sell copies of your book. Orchard Books put on a book launch for one of our readers, Fiona Dunbar (author of *The Lulu Baker Trilogy*), and it was spectacular. She'd written the last book in the trilogy and one of the themes that ran through it was magic and chocolate. It was held in a glamorous hotel with a high glass ceiling and we were served chocolates and strawberry liqueurs. The publisher made a speech, and it was a chance for Fiona to publicly thank everyone involved for all their support.

If you're publishing for the first time it would be a good idea to talk with a local bookseller about hosting a launch for you. If they have the space, it's in their interest to promote sales in this way. It's also a wonderful way to celebrate all your hard work, and if you manage to sell some copies then even better.

If your publisher has a publicity budget for your book

If you're already a best-seller or your publisher's creating a hype about your book then you may already have events lined up. If your publisher has arranged an author tour then be prepared for a punishing schedule. It may involve going around the country (even abroad) for radio and magazine interviews, TV, book signings, and a chance to meet booksellers. It's hard work but worthwhile.

For book reviews, publicity will send out copies of your book to magazine and newspaper editors. It's great if you can get a positive quote from a reviewer that could then be used on the jacket cover or for attracting foreign sales. Ignore bad reviews – you can't please everyone.

Your book is on the shelves

This is unlikely to attract a fanfare so don't feel neglected if this is the case, although some publishers will send flowers or a congratulatory card on the day of publication.

You should make it your own occasion, though. Go and check the bookshops – introduce yourself to the booksellers and bring their attention to your book. If you don't feel comfortable doing this take a friend so they can do it on your behalf. I remember going around with Lee after her third book was out and selling her unabashedly to any store we visited. The booksellers were happy to meet her and make her book more visible on the front table. Apart from celebrating, you need to sell copies, so anything that helps raise the profile of your book is good.

If you find your book isn't in a shop don't harangue sales in the publishing house, but you might draw up a list of stores that don't stock it or send a query email. Chain booksellers tend to buy centrally now rather than individual stores making their own decision on what they buy, so it may be that the central buyer for Waterstones didn't order your book.

Best-seller lists and blockbuster books

If your book is marketed well and has caught the buying mood of the public, your novel could well fly off the shelves. But how many copies have to be sold to make it into the best-seller charts? Figures that are based on quantities of sales and revenue are determined by EPOS (electronic point of sale) and are supplied by Nielsen BookScan. It produces a weekly list of the top 5,000, and this is referred to by publishers and retailers to monitor what's selling well (or not so well, which can be an instant death of a book) and what's in stock. On an average week (so not the weeks building up to Christmas, for instance) for hardback and paperback, your book would have to sell at least 110 copies to get into the top 5,000. To get into the top ten – the list that you might see in a weekend newspaper or a trade magazine – for hardback fiction it would need to sell 3,500 copies, for paperback fiction about 18,000 copies, and for overall children's (hardback and paperback) at least 3,500 copies.

Determining what is a best-seller can vary hugely as the figures depend upon how many other books have sold and the time of year. A book might shoot to number one and fade almost as quickly, or it might have sustained sales that turns it into a best-seller. Lists are often defined by genre and may be broken down into categories such as original fiction, mass-market fiction, fiction heatseekers (for instance, doing well but not in the top 20), and children's, and sometimes the figures are all combined – top 50 or top 100.

With in excess of 100,000 *new* books being published per year, to get anywhere near the best-seller list is a real achievement. If you're self-publishing your blockbuster, you won't want to miss out on being in the best-seller lists, so don't forget to log your ISBN number with Nielsen BookData so that they can track your book (see www.nielsenbookdata.co.uk for more information).

While Nielsen provide figures for newspapers such as the *Times* and the *Guardian*, the newspapers decide what to include in their lists. For instance, The Highway Code will sell consistently well every week, but that doesn't mean it will be included. The best resource for an author to refer to is *The Bookseller* trade magazine, which publishes a combined chart and the most overall comprehensive lists (see 'Taking it further').

Certain factors can also influence what makes a best-seller. If your book is a front-list title there will most likely be some form of marketing and advertising push, such as a poster campaign or a radio ad. Even if your book isn't front-list, word-of-mouth can be hugely effective and have a long-term impact. Good reviews, and having your book included in promotions such as part of a '3 for 2' Waterstones' offer, or simply having your book displayed on a table in a bookshop, will all aid sales. The biggest boost, that can turn a book into an overnight best-seller, is if it is reviewed by a high-profile bookclub, such as 'Richard & Judy'. If a supermarket stocks a title then that too can have an immense influence, particularly as they order a much smaller range in bulk compared to a mainstream retailer (although the high discount factor often means that there isn't much revenue to be recouped by the author and publisher).

Start your next novel

This is most likely underway already. In fact, it's a good idea to think about your next novel as you submit your first, to keep your spirits high and your mind distracted. So, by this stage you should have already started writing, and then the process begins again. This time, though, you will have your publisher (and agent if you have one) to help you on your way.

14

exploring other publishing avenues

In this chapter you will learn:
- about packagers, printers and self-publishers
- the pros and cons of self-publishing
- about writing schemes and online publishing.

Publishers versus packagers

If you have little or no luck with agents or editors you might want to think about getting in touch with a packager. The main one in the UK is Working Partners (WP), and it has an excellent reputation for launching first-time writers and building their career. They are also good gap fillers for published writers who find that they have a few months in between books.

WP devise concepts and storylines – for the children's and adult market – in the form of a synopsis and character list. They then invite authors, usually no more than six or seven, to produce a sample chapter(s) based on the specific brief. WP will then choose the appropriate author and the book or series will be submitted to leading English-language publishers, mainly in the UK and US.

If commissioned, you will receive a small advance set against a percentage of WP royalty income from the publisher. Whatever you do, do *not* send in your own submission with a synopsis and sample material. As they create their own storylines, to protect their integrity unsolicited submissions will be automatically disposed of. As a first step, you should go to the website and contact them by email or telephone. There is a form to fill out, and when a project is suitable to your experience and interest they will invite you to pitch. Every writer is considered and feedback is given on rejected samples. Bear in mind that 80% of authors they commission are via an agent. Don't go in it for the money, but do view it as a way that might get you started as a writer. (Check their website, www.working-partnersltd.co.uk, for more information.)

Do-it-yourself publishing

There are various options available to you:

- getting your book printed by a book printer
- self-publishing – companies that print your book and aid you through the publishing cycle
- writing schemes
- Internet/online publishing.

A word of warning: none of the above should be confused with vanity publishing – companies that promise to publish and sell your work when you pay them for this privilege (anything from

£1,000 to £10,000), and where you usually get very little in return. Despite promises to market and sell your book, more often, your books will languish in a warehouse. Some companies then offer to sell you back your book at a high cost per copy which means you've paid twice – once to get it published and again to buy back copies of your book – leaving little hope of making any profit. With the burgeoning trend for authors to self-publish and make a success of it, many vanity publishers are representing themselves as self-publishers, so you need to be vigilant if you are going it alone. Of course, no vanity publisher would ever call itself that – it's a label that those in the publishing world use.

The main way to identify a vanity publisher is by how much they charge and whether they retain the rights to exploit your work. Self-publishers, for instance, help you to get your book published for a fee but you retain all rights and income earned.

Some vanity publishers advertise in newspapers, magazines or on the web – 'authors wanted', etc. You may want to respond and ask for details, as some of these may be for companies that are not vanity publishers, and even if they are, some companies are better than others.

Study the contract and be suspicious of high fees and extra fees that reach into the £1000s. Even if they send you press releases of reviews and success stories and the contract seems watertight with promises of marketing and promotion, it's a good idea to investigate further if you are in any doubt. I often get calls from writers who have gone down the vanity route – one author even re-mortgaged her house to afford it – and then find that they make very little, if any, return from it. You may think this is naïve, but there are plenty of authors who fall into this trap.

My advice is to do your research and be ruthless with yourself. If you have to pay a publisher up front, where is their share of the risk and incentive to sell copies of your book? Also, when you pay a vanity publisher you will be granting them exclusive rights to publish your work and you might only expect to see token royalties and a token amount of free copies of your book. And remember, this right to publish may last the full length of copyright. Is the urge to see your name in print worth paying this much for so little in return?

Printing your book

You might want to consider printing or self-publishing if you've:

- written a niche book where you already know where and who to sell it to
- written one that won't necessarily have a mass-market appeal – perhaps a chapter book present for your grandchildren – and where you might expect to sell a few hundred copies in the local area and to family or friends
- become fed up with the trade not snapping up your book and you'd rather do it yourself, or you perhaps don't even want to go down the traditional route and would prefer to do it on your own anyway.

These are all good reasons for deciding to go it alone. But before you do, you should look at the pros and cons. You would have to do everything yourself from typesetting to selling it in to bookshops, which you might find fun and challenging, or time-consuming and exhausting. However, you would be looking at receiving a higher percentage in royalties: sometimes as high as 40% compared to the standard 10–15% from a publisher.

Given the revolutionary development of digital printing you can print as many or as few as you like and monitor your costs well. There is also print-on-demand (POD), an aspect of digital printing, which allows a book to be printed one at a time. A consumer can go into a bookshop and order your book, and you, your printer or self-publisher would then deliver to the bookshop within a few days. This technology allows you to mirror the sales demand and also eliminate the cost of warehousing, thereby making self-publishing potentially a more efficient and viable option.

Be prepared to *not* make any money from this. You need to take into account the overall cost of publishing your book and your time spent marketing, selling and publicizing. A bookshop may only buy your book at 40% of the RRP, and with that minus the printing costs and your overheads you might not make any profit.

If you are going to a printer for a one-off print run and it's not POD, who will distribute your books – will you? If so, how much will that cost and where will you store the copies? You could appoint a distributor (refer to the *Writers' and Artists' Yearbook* for guidance, or go online and identify a book distributor) but it's rare for them to take on a one-off author as they mainly distribute for publishers and wholesalers. If you do manage to get one, what will the distribution and warehouse costs be?

How many should you print? For conventional litho printing, the longer the print run the lower the unit cost per book, but you're taking more of a financial gamble if you don't sell all the copies. Digital printers advise an initially small print run – no more than 100–200 – and to use these to first sample the market. Bear in mind that some bookshops won't stock books from one-off authors, particularly those who don't have a distributor on board, so it's best to do the rounds of bookshops with a sample copy before you commit to a larger print run. Start with the booksellers in your area, in particular independent bookshops, as you will be speaking to the owner/manager who will be in charge of ordering. Chain booksellers tend to have a central buying policy where individual stores have little say over what they stock, so check if this is the case before you tantalize them with your book.

This initial print run should be used to send copies to newspapers, radio, TV, and writing magazines for review or interview. And of course free copies to close family – anyone else, including friends, should really buy the book, otherwise you may never make a profit. Once you have a feel for the market then you can order the next print run.

Printer, self-publisher or online publishing?

Once you've looked at the pros and cons and you decide that printing or self-publishing is for you, then you need to do some research. First, contact some printers – ones that specialize in printing books – and find out how they would want you to submit your book, what services they offer, the costs, and how much time it will take to see the book through the publishing process. There are many options, so choose one that matches your needs. The main difference is that if you're new to this, you may want to choose a self-publisher, or a combined printer and self-publisher, rather than a book printer in the first instance, as they'll be able to guide you through the publishing process.

Best-selling author Stephen Clarke went to a local digital printer in Paris. He started with 200 copies of *A Life in the Merde* and distributed them himself by hawking them to bookshops and sending them off direct to his web customers. He then did batches of 1,000 but stopped at 4,000 when his book sold to a publisher. This is his experience:

> *It was getting tough rereading proofs of each print run. Also, the books were expensive, around five euros each for the 1,000 print run (seven euros for the 200 run). I charged between £6.99 plus £3 postage for UK direct buyers of Merde ... to 12 euros plus three euros postage for French direct buyers. Obviously bookshops' discounts seriously dented my profits – although I charged more to those who refused me at first and then started to stock it when it began to take off. I never supplied on spec, I always insisted that a sale was a sale with a 30-day invoice, otherwise you can't manage your stock. It's a risk (that big publishers take), but I didn't want to be getting returns a year later. Only one little bookshop refused to work this way. It cost me a fortune to send the books to the UK, and there was a time deadline to respond to orders. I was losing money on each copy sold so I stopped supplying them. Even so, they carried on taking orders, which is why I went so high up the charts. In the end, I didn't mind the high costs because my intention always was to try and attract a major publisher.*

There is a book printers in the UK called Lightning Source, www.lightningsource.com, that primarily deals with trade publishers and wholesalers. They tend not to cater to the one-off-author but if you set up your own self-publishing company or your book is held by a self-publisher they will print and distribute for you. They expect you to be knowledgeable about the publishing business and are unlikely to explain in detail what you need and how to go about it.

Antony Rowe (AR), www.antonyrowe.co.uk, is a printer that deals with trade publishers, distributors and wholesalers but they also help publish one-off books and first time authors, so in many respects are part printer and part self-publisher. One of our authors, Sylvie Nichels, used them for *Another Kind of Loving*. The following is a breakdown of her costs.

Sylvie provided AR with the required final typeset format (a local designer did it for £100), she paid £150 for a publishing package which bought her the ISBN, sent out the legally required copies to British Library (and others), supplied wholesalers Gardners, and posted the title on Amazon and on AR's website. AR recommended an illustrator for her jacket cover (£240). The total production cost was £490. AR supplied her with a cost price per copy of £3.74 plus carriage (30 books per box); the RRP is £7.99; she charges £7 to friends but adds £1.50 to cover postage. Sylvie also spent £50 for promotional postcards and then fifteen pence per card. She uses these as one would a business card. If anyone is interested in buying a copy she gives them a card which has the cover design and ISBN number on it, she also leaves these in bookshops which is cheaper than leaving a speculative copy of the book. However, it's difficult to say how effective these cards are in converting into sales.

AR don't offer any help on marketing so this was down to her to set up. She gave talks at the Women's Institute and attended writing fairs, but she didn't want to trawl around every retailer promoting her book. Neither did she have a website, as she wasn't keen to go down this route (although I would strongly advise a website). Selling copies has been a slow process, but she has now covered her costs and at least her book's not languishing in the drawer.

The one disadvantage she found is that when people ask for her book in a bookshop it shows up as 'out of print' by the very nature that it's POD. Even though the book can be supplied within a few days, people find it off-putting. As a result, AR agreed with Gardners to hold ten copies, which means that it now shows up as being in print. All the structural, copy-editing and proofing was down to her, but if there is a typo AR will change it. This is the benefit of POD, but doesn't help if you already hold published copies. Sylvie says she would only encourage authors to go down this route if they're prepared to put in the leg-work.

There are a lot of online publishers, but one that's receiving attention at the moment is Lulu, an American site: www.lulu.com. It was set up by Bob Young, a technology entrepreneur, who had a less than positive experience with his non-fiction book when his publisher went out of business. This inspired him to create a POD publishing tool that allows authors to publish and sell their own books and e-books and other content products on the website. Lulu doesn't charge authors upfront, but charges a commission based on sales, which is 25% of the author's royalty. So, if you choose to make

£4 on your book Lulu will make £1. It started out in the US and 'holds' 45,000 titles with 1,200 new titles a week, and it's just expanding into the UK. If an order is placed on your book the printer takes 48 hours to print and bind it with a cover. This is then packaged and sent off or shipped. Within three days of being ordered it's in the mail.

Authors OnLine, www.authorsonline.co.uk, the company that founded digital printing, will, for a fee, convert your manuscript and cover for printing, provide you with an ISBN and send off the requisite copy to the British Library (and other legal deposit libraries – see Chapter 15 for more details). It will also make your book available to all retail outlets in the UK, US, North America, and Internet bookstores such as Amazon. On top of the unit cost of printing they will pay you 60% of the net revenue of all retail sales.

> The upside to POD is when you have a small print run for a standard sized book. The downside is that it costs one pence a page, so if your book is longer than 250 pages or you want a print run of more than 200 then it can be a more expensive option than litho printing.
>
> Richard Fitt, Director of Authors OnLine

They also offer a free service where they will do a print run of 30 books if you provide them with a typeset manuscript on a disk. This is without obligation to use their service. Of all the alternative publishers I looked into, Authors OnLine is the only one that has some form of quality control. They will look at sample chapters and will only accept a manuscript if it is up to a certain standard.

AuthorHouse, www.authorhouse.com, is a self-publishing company that offers a range of services to help you to market and publicize your book – you can even pay extra to get your book stocked in one of the main stores of a chain bookseller. Choose carefully which additional services you opt for as it can become expensive.

Grosvenor House Publishing (GHP) is another option. Author G. P. Taylor is the director of this company following his experience in self-publishing before he was taken on by Faber & Faber. GHP offer an all-round package for a fee, which includes guidelines on how to market and sell your book plus a free poster and business cards, a pre-designed jacket cover and a list of local newspapers and radio stations for you to contact. They offer additional services such as proofing and run retail marketing campaigns where your book is placed in 125 retailers for three months minimum across the country. Their website, www.selfpublishing.co.uk, is easy to follow and offers some good advice including costings and potential revenue.

There are many other self-publishers out there, with new ones emerging all the time. So, take your time in choosing and use the above as a guideline, and not as a definitive list.

Before you make a decision here's what you will need to consider:

- Get competitive **quotes** from a range of printers that specialize in printing books, or self-publishers.
- Decide which size and **format** to opt for – paperback, or hardback.
- Decide on a **recommended retail price** – look at comparable books.
- **Copy-edit, proofread** and **typeset** your manuscript – employ an editor if you're not confident about these aspects.
- Design your own **jacket** (or get a local designer to do it for you) – it should be of high quality as you don't want your book to look amateurish. You should have this a few months before the publication date so you can use if for promotional purposes. Don't forget to liaise with your printer on this issue.
- Write your **blurb**.
- Try to get an **author quote** to put on your jacket cover. Only do this if the author carries weight and is well known.
- Include your **website** and email address (on back of jacket).
- Register the **ISBN** (International Standard Book Number). Look up www.isbn.nielsenbookdata.co.uk for further information. You can apply for up to ten ISBN numbers at any one time for about £100. There is no time limit to use these. The ISBN number must appear on the title verso page (the same page that has your copyright notice and the printer's details) and above the barcode on the back of the book.

- You need a **barcode** if you are to sell your books. GS1 UK, www.gs1uk.org, is a standard organization and offers a free service to convert your ISBN number into a barcode and takes a matter of seconds. Once they've supplied the numbers your printer can then convert it into a barcode.
- Get a **publication date** (make sure your printer delivers on time).
- Start **publicizing** and **selling-in** your book to retailers.
- Send copies of your manuscript to **libraries**. Every published book within a month of publication needs to be sent to the British Library. This is a legal requirement under the deposit regulations of the Copyright Acts 1911 and 1963. You should also send a copy to: Bodleian Library, Oxford University Library, Cambridge National Library of Scotland Library of Trinity College, Dublin National Library of Wales Look up the British Library website www.bl.uk/contact/-howto.html for further information.

Self-publishing success stories

You would be in excellent company if you self-published: Virginia Woolf, James Joyce, Beatrice Potter, James Redfield and Thomas Hardy (even Stephen King published one of his later books on the net), and the list of famous authors goes on.

G. P. Taylor, who wrote *Shadowmancer*, self-published because he didn't want to go through the process of rejection by publishers. It sold so well that it was picked up by Faber & Faber. Although he pays no attention to best-seller lists, (in fact he says they irritate him as the figures are often unreliable), it went straight to the top.

> I self-published as a hobby and wanted to keep as much control as possible. I only expected my book to be read by a few people and was surprised when it took off.
>
> G. P. Taylor

Stephen Clarke had many rejections and false starts with the trade so he invented a trendy, young alter ego as the author which gave him a huge sense of freedom.

> I could write what I wanted, do the cover, everything and that sense of fun came through in the book. I had to start selling *Merde* door to door, from bookshop to bookshop. If it works, that's a great way to sell because it's true word-of-mouth – the best publicity – but I think lots of people give up, or don't have the courage to do it. It is very tough going into a bookshop and saying will you buy my book. Which is partly why I hid behind a character. I was saying, will you buy this book by this sexy young Brit I've discovered – big difference. [Transworld] found out about me because I was on Radio 4 talking about this English bloke living in Paris and writing funny things about the French and the MD emailed me that morning.
>
> Stephen Clarke

Macmillan new writing scheme

Macmillan has changed the way it views and processes unsolicited manuscripts and now has a dedicated imprint to new writing. It is for adult novels only, so no children's stories.

Contact them first on www.macmillannewwriting.com or call them for their terms and conditions as there are special submission criteria, such as only considering completed manuscripts. Every manuscript is considered and they commission about two books a month. If your book was taken on you wouldn't receive an advance (but neither do you pay anything to be published) but they do pay 20% of royalties and your book would remain in print for a minimum of two years.

They manage all the subsidiary rights to your book and have an option to publish your next book on the same terms as the first. They don't expect to make much profit from this scheme but they do believe in giving first-time authors a chance to be published. I think it's a great scheme and hope it succeeds – and better still, that other publishers will follow their example.

Goodwill to all authors?

A self-published book used to be considered a non-starter by the trade as it had already been exposed to a market. For instance, if an author had sold, say, 1,000 copies in a niche or local area, a publisher might be put off by the fact that a portion of the market had already been exposed to it. However, due to recent successes publishers are beginning to consider self-published books more seriously, and may commission those that sell well.

The ethos behind self-publishing is that everyone has the right to publish their book and the consumer will determine what they buy. However, as with most self-publishers and printers there is no structural, copy-editing or proofing attention. It's solely your responsibility to ensure that what you published is the best that it can be. While the public is more than ready to support authors who choose to go it alone, goodwill may soon wane if authors publish substandard work. Never forget that people buy books because they want to be entertained. If they buy a book that reads badly or is littered with mistakes it will not only be a waste of their money but their time. The doors are finally springing open for new writers but I worry that alternative publishing will get a bad name if there is not enough care over what is being released. Ultimately, though, word-of-mouth is the most powerful tool so if you self-publish, your stunningly well-written blockbuster will shine above the rest anyway.

Treat self-publishing as an exercise and a bit of a gamble if you can afford to, and any profit or success treat as a bonus.

15

troubleshooting

In this chapter you will learn:
• the answers to some
  frequently asked questions.

I've been told that my novel...

Has poor characterization. You may not know your characters well enough to bring them to life for others. Can you hear your characters talking in your head as you write (complete with different voices and styles of phrase), and do you think of them as real people? If not, you should have another go at the exercises in Chapter 02. Or, it might be that you're trying to control your characters' actions and force them to do things for the sake of your plot – this will turn the strongest characters flat. If this is the case, look at your synopsis or notecards again, and rethink them in terms of what your characters would actually do. Trust your characters, and let them lead the way.

Wanders aimlessly. Did you plan your story before you wrote it? This is often the culprit when a story has no sense of direction. Read Chapter 03 again, and make sure that your novel has both a strong action and emotional plot. Try putting your story on the three-act graph. Does it fit easily? Where does it lag? Work out how you can solve the problem areas, keeping cause and effect and escalating tension in mind. You might want to go back and work with your notecards or synopsis again, just to keep yourself on track.

Isn't emotionally involving. This comes down to your main characters. How well do you know them? Read Chapter 02 again. Are your main characters engaging, likable narrators? Do readers enjoy their company? If not, perhaps you know things about your characters that will make them more sympathetic that you could include, or perhaps you need to look at ways to make them more interesting to readers. It might be that your main characters remain static throughout the story, and don't undergo an emotional journey. Work through the character exercises again, and see how your characters could grow and change as a result of your action storyline. Finally, it might be that your characters don't have a pressing problem that will keep readers involved. Make sure that this element is in place, and that the problem is one that your characters care deeply about.

Is too complicated. This usually means that you're trying to cram too many storylines and/or characters into a single novel. Read the chapters on plot/scene structure (Chapter 03) and pacing (Chapter 08) again. Work out your main character(s) and storyline, and then look at everything else you have in place. Is all of it absolutely needed? Could you do without this subplot, that character? Kill your darlings and find ways to simplify, so that your main storyline has room to breathe.

Is too long. Overwriting and poor construction are usually the culprits. Have a look at Chapter 08 again, and ask yourself some hard questions. Is every scene needed? Are you getting into them late and out early, and constructing them around a central point of tension? Is your story filled with redundant or unnecessary information, overlong descriptions and/or endless character angst? All of these things will bog down a story considerably. Look at ways to tighten and trim, and be merciless with yourself: if it doesn't add to your story, it needs to go.

Is too passive. You're telling and not showing your action and characters to us. Have a read of Chapter 06 again, and go through the 'Action plan for active writing.'

Is boring. Several issues could be the problem here. Are your characters interesting, with vitally engaging problems? Make sure they have distinct emotional journeys that your readers can care about. Do your scenes have definite points of tension? Have you kept the story's stakes high, and made sure that tension keeps rising as the story goes along? Finally, look at your pacing. Your story should keep moving forward at a good pace, delving into the exciting scenes and speeding past the boring parts.

Feels rushed and 'thin'. A lack of show, don't tell will be one of the main problems, along with pacing issues. Read these chapters again for tips on how to slow your pace down and bring your story richly to life. Make sure that you're entering fully into your scenes as you write, living them along with your characters and striving to report them back to your reader as truthfully as you can.

Is derivative. Are you familiar enough with your genre? It might be that you've inadvertently trodden familiar ground through not being aware of what's already been done. If this is the case, take a few months off from writing and read everything you can find in your genre. Get used to its common themes and to what the trends are. Or, it might be that you've studied the market and are consciously trying to imitate someone else's blockbuster. Read Chapter 01 again if so. This never works – you need to find your own voice and your own ideas.

I've studied writing books – why can't I get published?

It's unlikely you'll succeed if you write by numbers, but writing courses and reading as much as you can in the genre you're writing in are excellent first steps. If you have talent, originality and believe passionately in what you're writing these are the essential ingredients to sparkling fiction.

However, not all talented writers can self-edit naturally, so without mastering these skills your writing will remain unshaped and possibly unpublished. As you begin to learn how to self-edit you'll start to know what to apply to your writing and what to disregard, and the process will become much easier, ideally taking your writing onto a new stage. The next step to getting published is to learn about the industry and how to submit in a professional way – and persevere. If you have your blockbuster then it will get noticed.

If I can't get my first book published what's the point in carrying on?

This is a common mistake that many first-time writers make. It doesn't mean that you can't write or will never get published: it may be that the market isn't ready for your book or that your writing needs to develop; your first book may even be published at a later date as book two or three. While we advocate revision you also have to know when to stop and begin another novel. If you're unconfident about whether you're on the right track this may also be the time to get another opinion. Your novel may be very good and the fact that you haven't attracted a publisher may simply be a reflection of the market. Whatever you do, don't wallow on your own on what you perceive as a failure. Use your support system. Artists aren't expected to paint their masterpieces in one go and without outside inspiration or assistance, so why should writers put this pressure on themselves?

How do I protect and copyright my work?

As soon as you've written something in the UK it is automatically in copyright and lasts for your lifetime and 70 years after that. It doesn't protect the idea, or the plot of the story, but it does protect the way the idea is expressed or presented, and the way you weave it all together. It would be hard for anyone to steal a story as so much of a novel is in the *expression* of the idea, but in any case you should always put on the title page of your manuscript a © sign with your name and date of writing (or date of publication). This is not legally needed but it's good to have it somewhere in your work and is particularly precautionary if your writing goes outside the UK. See www.copyright.gov for more information.

Some authors like to log a hard copy. The best and cheapest way to claim ownership of your work is to package up your manuscript, seal it properly with tape and send it to yourself, register post. It must show the date, and remain unopened. Or you can put it in a safety deposit box in a bank or log it with your solicitor. There are companies that deposit your work for an annual fee but usually any of the above is enough. This is different in the US where you will need to register your work as proof of ownership. See the UK www.patent.gov.uk for more information.

Never give up ownership of copyright (some vanity publishers ask for full copyright – see Chapter 14 for more information). For instance, when your book is published you grant that publisher a licence to use your works that usually lasts for 25 years, and that can then be renegotiated. If your book goes out of print the publisher will notify you of this and will offer a 'reversion of rights' which then allows you to offer the licence to another publisher.

Even if you have registered or trademarked a name or a character *never* put ® or ™ marks on your manuscript as it will look amateurish.

What are PLR and ALCS?

PLR stands for public lending right, and is a government scheme whereby authors are paid a small sum every time one of their books is checked out of a library. The average payment per book loan is around five pence, which may not sound like much, but it can seriously add up: some authors earn the maximum PLR sum of £6,000 yearly, and most earn at least a few hundred pounds. You must register all of your published titles (including new editions) with PLR to receive payment for them:

Public Lending Right
Richard House
Sorbonne Close
Stockton-on-Tees TS17 6DA
Tel: 01642 604699

You can also register via their website: www.plr.uk.com

ALCS stands for Authors' Licensing and Collection Society, an organization that aims to ensure writers are fairly compensated for any of their works that are copied, broadcast or recorded. Similar to PLR, they pay out an annual sum to authors from a central fund. Payments tend to be smaller than PLR, but it's money you wouldn't have had otherwise, and well worth registering for. Again, you need to register all of your published titles, including new editions, to receive payment:

ALCS Ltd
Marlborough Court
14–18 Holborn
London EC1N 2LE
Tel: 020 7395 0600

You can also download a registration form via their website: www.alcs.co.uk

I've used lines from famous songs – do I need permission?

If you want to quote a line from a song or quote from a book, if copyright is still active then you need to write to the publisher or author for permission. It is your responsibility to do this and you will also have to bear any cost for the right to use it (and using a song can be expensive). In some cases, your publisher may contribute to the costs but this is rare. If you don't hear from either party (or whoever holds the rights to that work) then flag it up with your publisher as permission outstanding when you submit your novel. They should then confirm whether it's necessary to pursue it or not.

There are exceptions according to the length of the quote used. For instance, if you quote a sentence and make reference to the source you may not need permission. Your publisher should guide you on this but if you're in any doubt try and get permission anyway.

Will I be sued for libel?

Libel is what you write, and it shouldn't be confused with slander which is what you say. If you write about someone in a defamatory way where it could damage their work or personal reputation then you may end up being sued, the costs of which you may have to bear yourself. Sometimes a publisher steps in to support you but they're not obliged to do so. Some publishers have in-house lawyers where they check for murky areas before a book is published but the onus really is on you to either disguise your character extremely well or to make sure that what you write is true.

For instance, if one of your characters is a shady dealing owner of a recognizable company (with a mere name change), just changing his physical description is probably not enough. If you write about a public figure in a derogatory way, which is based on hearsay rather than first-hand fact, then you're in trouble if you can't back up your claim. If you write a sizzling novel where your love-rat character is *loosely* based on your neighbour, then be prepared to defend the fact that while you may have borrowed a detail from him (such as pacing around the garden in his blue, silk dressing gown as he's on his mobile phone), the rest of the character is wholly fictitious.

There have been cases where even if the writer is innocent to any connection, the fact that a person might be recognized or a link made in a damaging way makes this a potential problem. If you've written about a lawyer, doctor, builder, car mechanic, etc. in a defamatory way check that there is no person or company in the UK that bears or even resembles the name that you've used. If you do end up being sued for libel it would be up to the person accusing you to prove that what you wrote wasn't true, not up to you to prove that it was, but it's still not worth the risk.

An identical story to mine has just been published

This is really bad luck and unfortunately not uncommon. One journalist told me she was about to write a story set around the slave trade era, based on a primary source that had never been written about before. A week later a book came out using that same story. Luckily she was only at proposal stage so hadn't wasted significant time on it. You can't safeguard against writing a book that is very similar to another, especially if it comes out at the same time; all you can do is put it behind you and begin again if this happens. If there's any question of plagiarism, so long as you can prove that you didn't set out to copy the story (see 'copyright' section), you should be fine.

An author friend recommended I contact a publisher – how do I mention this?

This is plain nepotism and I would highly recommend it. No one in the trade would like to admit that this would make a difference, but it does, and you should use it to your advantage. If you know an author, or someone put you in touch with an agent or publisher, say so in your cover letter (though do check with the person first that it's OK to mention their name) – preferably at the beginning, as it may put your submission at the top of the pile.

However, don't make it up, or make out that you know the person well when you only briefly talked to them at a party. It would be awful for an agent to talk to that person, mention your name and for them to not know who you are! Also, be aware that an introduction will only bring your submission to an agent or editor's attention. If your story isn't good enough or doesn't appeal then it will still get rejected.

afterword

When we sent out questionnaires to writers, agents and publishers – many of whom are quoted throughout this book – one of the questions to the trade was, 'Is it easier now than it was five years ago for first-time writers to get published?'

The response was a resounding 'no'. The market is tougher than ever. This fact has been largely determined by the increasing power of bookshop chains, by centralized buying, and by sales data from EPOS – which can make or break a book within weeks. As a result, publishers are finding it increasingly hard to place books and to make any profit. The objective side to this argument is that retailers are driven by consumer demand and competitive pricing, where they have to compete with supermarkets and online retailers. Nevertheless, editors have to trim their lists and favour established sellers, even though it may not be the publishing ethos that they favour.

> In my view, there is far too much concentration on the new, on the 'latest sensation' and not nearly enough on the long-term development of the craft of writing. In my experience, writers get better and better over time. Sometimes they need one or two not-so-good books to be published just to give them the impetus to write the masterpiece. This seems to demand a much more forgiving book world than the one we have at present but I am not without hope that the human desire for narrative and story will change this.
>
> David Fickling, David Fickling Books

However, all agreed that even though it's tougher to get published now, if a novel really stands out then it's going to get noticed. The discovery of a new writer who crackles with promise is always going to be exciting, and it is important for writers to take heart from this.

Lastly, a writer should never lose sight as to why we all like to read books. Quite simply, if it's a damn good read and it connects with the reader – be it for the writing style, exploratory themes, tight plot, strong characters, or racing pace – then it will get noticed and deserves to succeed.

We hope this book goes some way towards demystifying the process of writing commercial fiction and submitting it to the trade in a professional way. We wish all you future blockbuster writers well, and look forward to hearing about your successes, even if it's just the fact that you love to write. Writing a novel is a huge achievement in itself, and that to us is the first and lasting success.

Helen Corner
Lee Weatherly

taking it further

Recommended reading

Books

Bell, J. (ed) (2001) *The Creative Writing Coursebook*, Pan Macmillan.
An amalgamation of writer tips, exercises and case studies, used by creative writing MA students at the UEA.

Blake, C. (1999) *From Pitch to Publication*, Pan Macmillan.
A definitive reference by a leading UK agent, Carole Blake of Blake, Friedman Literary Agency. This is excellent if you want to understand contracts in detail.

Brande, D. (1934) *Becoming a Writer*, Pan Macmillan.
A classic guide for getting into the writer's mind.

Card, O. S. (1990) *How to Write Science Fiction and Fantasy*, Writer's Digest Books.
A classic reference by the Nebula and Hugo-winning author, Orson Scott Card.

Curtis, R. (1996) *How To Be Your Own Literary Agent*, Houghton Mifflin.
Written by an American agent for the US market.

King, S. (2001) *On Writing*, New English Library.
Excellent tips and insights from Stephen King – a master of blockbuster fiction.

Legat, M. (1998) *An Author's Guide to Publishing*, Hale.
Packed with information on the publishing process.

McCallum, C. (2003) *The Writers' Guide to Getting Published*, How To Books.
A broad outline on how to get published in book form, or write for magazines, radio and TV.

The Writers' & Artists' Yearbook, A&C Black.
Published annually, this is an invaluable reference, listing agents, publishers, media contacts, writing competitions, available grants, courses, and much more. It's packed with excellent advice for new authors and is used widely by the trade.

The Writer's Handbook, Macmillan.
An excellent all-round reference book for writers.

Magazines

The Author
84 Drayton Gardens
London SW10 9SB
Tel: 020 7373 6642
www.societyofauthors.org
info@societyofauthors.org
The Society of Authors' quarterly publication, comes free with membership.

The Bookseller
Tower Publishing Services
Tower House
Sovereign Park
Market Harborough
Leicestershire LE16 9EF
Tel: 01858 438841
The leading trade magazine of the publishing world, published weekly. You can also subscribe to their online edition at www.thebookseller.com.

Mslexia
Mslexia Publications Limited
PO Box 656
Newcastle upon Tyne NE99 1PZ
Tel: 0191 261 6656
www.mslexia.co.uk
A quarterly magazine for women writers featuring high-quality fiction, contests, writing tips.

Writers' Forum
Writers International Ltd
PO Box 3229
Bournemouth BH1 1ZS
Tel: 01202 589828
www.writers-forum.com
A monthly magazine for beginners as well as established writers.
Monthly tips, information on contests, courses, etc.

Writers' News and *Writing*
Freepost PE211
Bourne
Lincolnshire PE10 9BR
www.writersnews.co.uk

Writers' News comes free with your subscription to *Writing,*
which is one of the UK's leading writing magazines. It offers
monthly tips, information on contests, courses, etc.

Useful organizations

The Arts Council of England
14 Great Pover Street
London SW1P 3NQ
Tel: 0845 300 6200
www.artscouncil.org.uk
This is the national development agency for the arts in England.
Grants are sometimes available to new writers. Offices are
divided by area. Check their website to find your local division
along with contact details.

The Arts Council of Northern Ireland
77 Malone Road
Belfast BT9 6AQ
Tel: 0903 85200
www.artscouncil-ni.org

The Arts Council of Wales
9 Museum Place
Cardiff CF10 3NX
Central Office Tel: 029 20 376500
South Wales Office Tel: 029 20 376525
www.artswales.org.uk

The Scottish Arts Council
12 Manor Place
Edinburgh EH3 7DD
Help Desk: 0845 603 6000
www.scottisharts.org.uk

Association of Authors' Agents (AAA)
15 Britannia Street
London WC1X 9JN
Tel: 020 7833 0777
www.writersguild.org.uk
admin@writersguild.org.uk
This maintains a code of working practice for literary agencies
that are members.

The British Fantasy Society
www.britishfantasysociety.org.uk
Promotes fantasy, science fiction and horror. Holds an annual
conference open to both published and non-published authors.

The Children's Writers and Illustrators Group (CWIG)
The Society Of Authors (SOA)
84 Drayton Gardens
London SW10 9SB
Tel: 020 7373 6642
www.societyofauthors.net
info@societyofauthors.net
A branch of the Society of Authors. You must be a published
children's author or illustrator to join. CWIG also hold a semi-
annual conference open to both published and non-published
authors.

The Crime Writers' Association
www.thecwa.co.uk
For published crime writers. No central office or phone number,
if interested contact their website (includes information on
crime-writing festivals).

The Romantic Novelists' Association
38 Stanhope Road
Reading
Berkshire RG2 7HN
www.rna-uk.org
For both published and unpublished authors of romantic
fiction. Includes information on conferences and seminars.

The Society of Authors (SOA)
84 Drayton Gardens
London SW10 9SB
Tel: 020 7373 6642
www.societyofauthors.net
info@societyofauthors.net
You must be a published author or illustrator to join, and you can only become a member once you have a publishing contract. An excellent support service for authors; highly recommended.

The Society of Children's Book Writers and Illustrators
8271 Beverly Boulevard
Los Angeles
CA 90048
USA
Tel: 001 323 782 1010
www.scbwi.org
An American-based organization for both published and unpublished children's writers. The website is an excellent resource; they also run workshops and seminars. There's an annual fee to join.

The Writers' Guild of Great Britain
15 Britannia Street
London WC1X 9JN
Tel: 020 7833 0777
www.writersguild.org.uk
admin@writersguild.org.uk

This is the writers' trade union and affiliated to the TUC, and represents writers of books, film, TV, theatre and radio. You can only become a member once you have a written contract.

Useful websites

www.writers-circles.com
The directory of Writers' Circles, Courses and Websites provides a wealth of information, with a written guide also available for a small fee.

www.writewords.org.uk
WriteWords is a comprehensive online resource for writers that includes discussion forums, site experts, and a directory of agents, publishers, and useful links. There's an annual fee to join, though you can have a trial week's membership free.

Writing courses

The Arvon Foundation
Main Office: 42a Buckingham Palace Road
London SW1W 0RE
www.arvonfoundation.org
Well-established residential writing courses in all different genres, specific to creative writing. The Arvon Foundation run four centres throughout the UK. Check their website for details or ring/write for a brochure.

Cornerstones & Kids' Corner
Milk Studios
34 Southern Row
London W10 5AN
Tel: 0208 968 0777
www.cornerstones.co.uk
Popular and recognized courses on writing, self-editing, and submitting to agents. Held in Oxfordshire. Also offer online tutorials.

Loutro Writers
12 Vale Road
Bowden
Cheshire WA14 3AQ
Tel: 0161 928 5768
www.worldspirit.org.uk
Poetry and writing courses in an exotic Crete setting.

Ty Newydd
Llanystumdwy
Cricieth, Gwynedd
LL52 0LW
Tel: 01766 522 811
www.tynewydd.org
The national writers' centre for Wales offers well-established residential courses.

Writers' groups

The National Association of Writers' Groups
<u>www.nawg.co.uk</u>
Find a writers' group in your area. Includes an excellent, very comprehensive 'Links for Writers' section.

index